Handshake

a course in communication

Student's book ●

PETER VINEY & KAREN VINEY

Oxford University Press 1996

Contents

CONTENTS

For the student: Asking for help

formulas: can, could, do

Here are some formulas for asking for help:

Introducing the formulas
Sorry... / Excuse me ... / Pardon me ...

Formulas
Can you speak more slowly, please?
I don't understand.
Could you repeat that?
Could you explain *request*?
What does *request* mean?
What's (...) in English?
How do you say (...) in English?
How do you spell that?
How do you pronounce this word?

You can find definilions of key words in the Glossary on page 174.

Conversations

would like

quantity

what make / size?

A: Would you like a drink?
B: A mineral water, please.
A: Still or sparkling?
B: Still, please. And no ice.

> *fruit juice – orange or grapefruit*
> *some wine – white or red*

C : Can I help you?
D: Please. Some of this ... thank
   you ... and some of that, too.
C : Anything else?
D: Yes. One of those, and some of
   these. Thanks.

> *two of these*
> *a little of that*
> *a few of those*
> *some of this*

E: I'd like a film, please.
F: What size?
E: 35 millimetre. 24 exposure.
F: What make?
E: One of those.
F: There you go. One Agfa 35/24.

> *some cassettes*
> *C90*
> *five of these*
> *five Sony CR90s*

*This means
the dialogues
or texts are
recorded.*

 Listen to the conversations. Practise in pairs, then role-play
the conversations, using the words in the boxes.

Requests

degrees of politeness

can, may, could

intonation

1 Request formulas

Here are some formulas for requests. Which requests are formal? Which are informal?

not polite
Give me a coffee.
I want a coffee.

neutral
Coffee, please.
I'd like a coffee, please.
Can I have a coffee, please?

more polite
Could I have a coffee, please?
May I have a coffee, please?

very polite
I wonder if I could have a coffee, please.

2 Matching

Match the requests with the pictures.

A Excuse me, I wonder if I could see the menu, please.
B May I have the menu, please?
C Bring me a menu, please!

3 Intonation

You can find transcripts of listening sections in the Listening appendix, starting on page 166.

 Check your answers with the recording. Sometimes the intonation of a request is more important than the formula that you use. You can say *Give me a coffee* in a friendly tone of voice, and you can say *I wonder if I could have a coffee, please* in an impolite or unfriendly tone of voice.

4 Intonation: requests or commands?

Listen to these twelve sentences. Which of them sound like polite requests (*R*), and which sound like commands (*C*)? Listen and write *R* or *C*. Check with the Listening appendix. Remember, it's the intonation not the choice of formula that is important.

1	5	9 .....
2	6	10 .....
3	7	11 .....
4	8	12 .....

5 Pair Work

In your language, do you use tone of voice in a similar way?

Practise using the request formulas in **1**. Choose a formula and say it in one of these ways:
– as a command
– in a neutral way
– very politely

Ask your partner to guess your tone of voice. Repeat this with the other request formulas. You needn't request the same thing every time.

 See Active Grammar
requests

This means you can find more information in the Active Grammar appendix, starting on page 144.

If you don't know the words

demonstratives
mass and unit
food

1 A breakfast buffet

Sometimes we don't know the English word.
So, we can point and say:

This one, please.   *Some of this, please.*
That one, please.   *Some of that, please.*
Two of these, please.   *Some of these, please.*
Three of those, please.   *Some of those, please.*
The blue one, please.   *The red ones, please.*

 See Active Grammar
determiners

2 Asking for things

Practise asking for things from the buffet. If
you don't know the word, point and use *this /
that / these / those.*

3 Matching

Match the pictures to the items.

A	plates	N	rolls
B	coffee	O	bacon
C	yoghurts	P	cheese
D	cornflakes	Q	Rice Crispies
E	scrambled egg	R	tea
F	boiled eggs	S	sausages
G	Danish pastries	T	cups
H	mushrooms	U	toast
I	tomato juice	V	muesli
J	milk	W	ham
K	glasses	X	bread
L	jars of jam	Y	packets of butter
M	orange juice	Z	sugar

4 Working with words

Which of these words did you know?
Which ones did you guess?
Which ones are the same (or nearly the same)
in your language?
What do you have for breakfast?
Do you know what people in other countries
have for breakfast?

5 Countable or uncountable?

In dictionaries, you see *C* for countable things
and *U* for uncountable things.

Look at the list again, and write *C*, *U* or *C / U*
next to the words.

 See Active Grammar
countable / uncountable nouns

6 Asking for things again

Practise asking for things from the buffet
again. This time, you know the words. You
don't need *this / that / these / those*.

Room service

food
requests

1 Listening

This is an order form for room service breakfast. It's 7 a.m. Someone is telephoning a room service order. Tick (✓) their choices.

2 After you listen

Turn to the Listening appendix.
Underline all the requests in the transcript of the conversation.

3 Role-play

Role-play a conversation with room service. Order a large breakfast.

GRAND HOTEL
ROOM SERVICE BREAKFAST

BEFORE 6 a.m. *hang this order form on your door handle*
AFTER 6 a.m. *telephone for room service on 321*

CONTINENTAL BREAKFAST – £7.00

Juices
☐ orange   ☐ grapefruit   ☐ tomato

Hot drinks
☐ coffee   ☐ chocolate
☐ tea with milk   ☐ tea with lemon

Cereals
☐ cornflakes   ☐ Rice Crispies   ☐ muesli

Yoghurt
☐ strawberry   ☐ plain   ☐ peach melba

Bread and pastries
☐ White bread   ☐ Wholewheat bread
☐ White toast   ☐ Wholewheat toast   ☐ rolls
☐ croissants   ☐ Danish pastries
☐ doughnuts

Fruit
☐ apple   ☐ pear   ☐ banana   ☐ orange

COOKED BREAKFAST – £12.00
Continental breakfast plus:

Eggs
☐ fried   ☐ scrambled   ☐ boiled
☐ poached

plus
☐ bacon   ☐ sausages   ☐ tomatoes
☐ fried bread   ☐ mushrooms

All orders plus 15% service.   *VAT included*

ROOM NO: ....   NAME: ....

Requesting for others

I'd like

for + object
pronouns

1 He'd like the steak …

 How do you request things for other
people?

WAITER Are you ready to order?
WOMAN Yes, please.
WAITER Would you like a starter?
WOMAN No, thanks.
WAITER And for the main course?
WOMAN He'd like the steak, and she'd like
the fish. That's right, isn't it?
GUESTS Mmm / Yes.
WOMAN And they would both like the salad.
WAITER Fine. And what would you like,
madam?
WOMAN I'd like the chicken. And can you
bring us a bottle of white wine?
WAITER Certainly.

2 It's for her …

 What happens when the food arrives?

WAITER Who's the steak for?
WOMAN The steak's for him.
WAITER And the fish?
WOMAN That's for her.
WAITER And the two salads?
WOMAN The salads are for them. And the
chicken's for me.
WAITER There you go. Is that everything?
WOMAN Yes, that's all. Thank you.
WAITER You're welcome.

The Interaction appendix is at the back of the book. It begins on page 133.

3 Interaction

 You are going to do two role-plays. Turn to
the Interaction appendix.
Student A: look at section 3.
Student B: look at section 22.

 See Active Grammar
object pronouns

Culture comparison

Sunday Gazette 13 May   *Travel page*

DON'T WORRY– JUST SMILE!

You don't speak the language? Don't worry, just smile! That's what the experts on communication skills are saying. It's easy to communicate when you travel abroad. Smile, look at people in a friendly way and point at things and people will understand you. Or will they? People in different countries request things in different ways.

- ✪ The British say 'please' and 'thank you' more than the Americans. When they buy something the British may say 'thank you' two or three times during the conversation. The Americans say 'thank you' once.
- ✪ Americans always reply 'you're welcome' after 'thank you'. The British sometimes reply 'thank you', or sometimes do not reply.
- ✪ In Northern European countries (e.g. Scandinavia, The Netherlands, Poland and Germany), people request things simply and directly and their intonation sounds like an English command.
- ✪ In Southern Europe, a smile, friendly body language and eye contact are very important when you're requesting something.
- ✪ In Asia, people sometimes give a very small bow and often look away when requesting something.

Discuss

Which of the things below are important in your country when you're requesting something?
- smiling
- friendly body language
- eye contact
- polite formulas
- polite intonation

Countable and uncountable nouns

See Active Grammar

countable / uncountable nouns

1 Countable or uncountable?

Write *(C)* for countable and *(U)* for uncountable next to these words.

..... water	..... glasses of water
..... oil	..... litres of oil
..... bread	..... slices of bread
..... gold	..... grams of gold
..... meat	..... pieces of meat
..... shampoo	..... bottles of shampoo
..... pasta	..... bowls of pasta

Then make sentences.

There is some water. / There isn't any water.
There are some glasses of water. / There aren't any glasses of water.

2 Uncountable nouns

All the nouns in this list are uncountable in English. Compare the list with translations into your language. Does your language have countable and uncountable words? If so, are these countable *(C)* words, or uncountable *(U)*, in your language?

..... accommodation	..... money
..... advice	..... news
..... water	..... permission
..... bread	..... rice
..... furniture	..... spaghetti
..... gas	..... traffic
..... hair	..... travel
..... information	..... weather
..... luggage	..... work

3 Drinks

Water is uncountable, glasses of water are countable. When we ask for drinks, we say:

Two coffees, please. / I'd like a mineral water. / A beer, please.

This is because we are thinking of a cup of coffee, or a bottle of mineral water. If someone has a jug of water, or a large coffee pot, we ask for *some* water or *some* coffee.

Are these sentences correct (✔) or not (✘)?

1 Can you give me a tea, please?
2 There's a tea in the pot.
3 Would you like a beer?
4 Would you like some beer?

4 Indefinite articles and numbers

We don't usually put indefinite articles (*a / an*) or numbers (*two, five* etc.) with uncountable nouns. Choose the correct answers.

1 It's (a long / long) journey.
2 (Travel / A travel) helps you to understand other cultures.
3 We can find (accommodation / an accommodation) in the next town.
4 There's (a plate / plate) on the table.
5 She's got chicken. Put (a rice / rice) on her plate too.
6 I've got (a bad / bad) news.
7 That's (a good / good) advice.
8 You can find (an information / information) in the guide book.

5 Plural nouns

Some nouns only have a plural form, and you use plural words with them.

Those clothes aren't expensive.
Some United Nations troops were in the area.

You can have *a sock* or *two socks* or *a pair of socks*, but you can't have *a tight*, so *tights* always has an *-s* ending.

Underline the nouns which always have an *-s* ending.

socks	trousers	scissors
shoes	jeans	glasses
tights	shorts	earrings
trainers	pyjamas	underpants

Note: You can use *a pair of* with all the plural nouns above.

I've got a pair of sunglasses in my car.
I'd like a new pair of earrings.

Using quantity expressions

1 Singular or plural verbs?

Choose the correct form of the verbs.

1 There (isn't / aren't) enough milk in my coffee.
2 There (isn't / aren't) enough seats on the bus. We'll have to stand up.
3 There (was / were) plenty of time.
4 The theatre isn't full. There (is / are) plenty of seats left.
5 A lot of information (come / comes) from the Internet.
6 There (is / are) a lot of hotels in London.
7 How much money (is / are) there?
8 How many programs (is / are) there on your computer?
9 There (is / are) only a little accommodation at the university.
10 These cups (have / has) got coffee in them. Can you wash them again?
11 (Is / Are) there any scissors in your office?
12 Your luggage (hasn't / haven't) got a label.
13 These jeans (don't / doesn't) have a price tag. How much are they?
14 There (was / were) some rice in the pan.

2 Quantity words

Write C (always countable), U (always uncountable), or C/U (countable and uncountable) next to these quantity words.

..... plenty   ..... enough
..... much   ..... many
..... some   ..... a little
..... a lot   ..... a few

3 More work on singular and plural

Here are some sentences from a conversation in a restaurant. Choose the correct words.

1 'Do you like chicken?' 'Yes, I love (it / them).'
2 'More soup, madam?' 'Yes, please. (It's / They're) excellent.'
3 'Would you like more meat?' Yes, I'd like (some / one).'
4 'Would you like (a / any) more macaroni?' 'No, thanks.'
5 'My steak's cold.' 'Sorry, I'll change (it / them).'
6 '(This / These) rice comes with the meal.'
7 'I'd like some of (that / those) vegetables, please.'
8 'I'd like (three / some) ice-cream.'

4 Other problems with nouns

Here are some plural nouns ending in -s:

arms (= weapons)	*stairs*
troops (= soldiers)	*thanks*
congratulations	*clothes*
customs (at an airport)	*contents*

Here are some irregular plural nouns:

cattle   *children*   *people*   *police*

Here are some uncountable nouns which end in -s:

economics	*physics*
mathematics	*politics*
(social) studies	

Choose the correct words.

1 Physics (is / are) my favourite subject.
2 The police (was / were) in the street.
3 The stairs (is / are) made of wood.
4 She has a degree in (a European / European) Studies.
5 There (was / were) a lot of people at the concert.
6 The contents of the book (is / are) interesting.
7 The children (is / are) eating lunch.

5 Learning to learn

When you learn new nouns, write C for countable or U for uncountable next to them in your notebook. Look in a dictionary for more information.

greeting
formulas

dictionary skills

Greetings

1 Listening

How do people greet each other?
Listen to these conversations.

A: Angie! Great to see you again.
B: Great to see you.
A: How're you doing?
B: OK!

C: Hi, Mark ... Hi, Lucy. Nice to see you.
D: Nice to see you too. How's Amanda?
C: Oh, she's very well, thank you.

E: Good morning, Lisa.
F: Good morning, Ms Stewart.

G: Hello, Bob. How are you?
H: Fine thanks. And you?
G: Fine.

I: Good evening.
J: Good evening, sir ...
   madam. Welcome to the
   Chelsea International Hotel.

See Active Grammar
greeting formulas

2 Pair work

Practise the conversations.

3 Relationships

Read the definitions and discuss these
questions with your partner.
– Are the people in the conversations friends,
  relatives, acquaintances, co-workers or
  strangers?
– Is the language formal or informal?
– When do you *use* formal greetings?

---

acquaintance /əˈkweɪntəns/ noun [C] a person
that you know but who is not a close friend.
co-worker /ˈkəʊ wɜːkə(r)/ noun [C] (*Brit*
colleague) a person that you work with in a job.
formal /ˈfɔːml/ adj used about language or
behaviour when you want to appear serious or
official. The opposite is **informal.**
friend /frend/ noun [C] a person that you know
and like (not a member of your family).
relative /ˈrelətɪv/ noun [C] a member of your
family.
stranger /ˈstreɪndʒə(r)/ noun [C] a person that
you do not know.

cultural
awareness

present simple

Culture questionnaire

Complete the questionnaire, then compare your answers with a
partner. You may tick more than one box.

1 When do acquaintances shake hands in
your country?
☐ they don't shake hands at all
☐ every time they meet during a day
☐ when they meet for the first time
during a day
☐ when they say goodbye

2 When do people bow in your country?
☐ they don't bow
☐ they bow only to Heads of State
☐ they bow to superiors
☐ they bow to customers
☐ acquaintances bow when they meet

3 Which of these groups hug?
☐ no one hugs
☐ women hug women
☐ men hug women, women hug men
☐ men hug men
☐ adults hug children

4 Which people kiss each other when they
meet in your country?
☐ no one kisses in public in my country
☐ close relatives
☐ people in love
☐ good friends
☐ acquaintances
☐ colleagues
☐ strangers

5 A man meets a woman business friend.
What happens?
☐ they don't kiss
☐ they kiss once (on one cheek)
☐ they kiss twice (once on each cheek)
☐ they kiss three times on the cheeks
☐ they kiss on the lips
☐ he kisses her hand

Introducing yourself

© 1991 FarWorks, Inc.

1   Someone whose name you don't know

When you introduce yourself to a stranger, you usually do these four things:

A   greet them

B   say your name

C   give extra information (e.g. job, where you're from)

D   say something pleasant

Write *A*, *B*, *C*, or *D* beside each expression, as in the example.

..*B*.   I'm Annette Preston.

.....   Nice to meet you.

.....   I'm the Sales Manager of Greystoke Inc.

.....   How do you do.

.....   My name's McCartney. Paul McCartney.

.....   Hello.

.....   It's a pleasure to meet you.

.....   I'm a friend of Mrs Pickering.

.....   I'm very pleased to meet you.

.....   Let me introduce myself, I'm Sally Clark.

.....   I work for Dashwood Communications.

.....   I'm from Australia.

2   Someone whose name you know

Often we know someone's name before we meet them, so we check the name. The easiest way of checking someone's name is to say the name with a rising intonation:

Mr Porter?

 Listen to the recording and copy the intonation.

Mr Porter?

Ms Wilson?

John Brown?

Antonia?

3   Group work

Go around the class. You know people's names, but imagine that it's your first meeting. Check their names, using a rising intonation, then introduce yourself.

Introductions

HOW TO BE *successful* IN LIFE

Dr Lauren K. Beckenbauer

INTRODUCTIONS

Introducing yourself ~

☞ Shake hands firmly, and look the other person straight in the eye. Smile!
- Men shake hands with men.
- Women choose whether to shake hands with men or not. The woman offers her hand first.
- Nowadays women often shake hands with women (but not always).

☞ Say 'How do you do.' In the USA the response is 'Pleased to meet you,' or 'Fine, thanks.' In Britain, the response is usually 'How do you do.'

☞ Give information about yourself.
- State your name.
- Add extra information (job, company or where you live).

☞ Exchange business cards.

Introducing other people ~

☞ Introduce in the correct order.
- Introduce lower status to higher status.
- Introduce younger people to older people.
- Introduce men to women.

1 Reading

Read this extract from a magazine article.

2 Rules

Close the book, and make a list of the rules that you can remember. Compare your list with your partner.

3 Culture comparison

Discuss these rules with your partner.
- Are these rules true for your country?
- Were they more important in the past?
- Are rules still important nowadays?
- Do you prefer having rules, or not?

4 Find the conversations

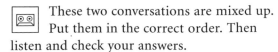 These two conversations are mixed up. Put them in the correct order. Then listen and check your answers.

1 How do you do, Nick.
Mr Granger, I'd like you to meet Nick Thomas, from our Boston office.
Please. Call me Philip.
Pleased to meet you, Mr Granger.

2 I'm Paul Hodges from Warner Graphics.
How do you do.
Yes.
Sarah Dean?
Would you like to see our new catalogue?
How do you do.

Introducing other people

present simple
to be
how old?

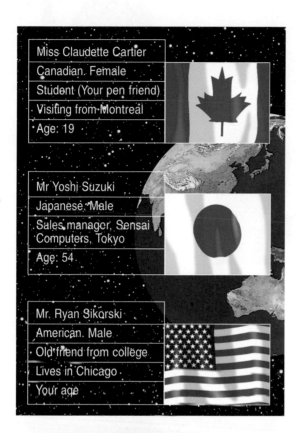

Miss Claudette Cartier
Canadian. Female
Student (Your pen friend)
Visiting from Montreal
Age: 19

Mr Yoshi Suzuki
Japanese. Male
Sales manager, Sensai Computers, Tokyo
Age: 54

Mr. Ryan Sikorski
American. Male
Old friend from college
Lives in Chicago
Your age

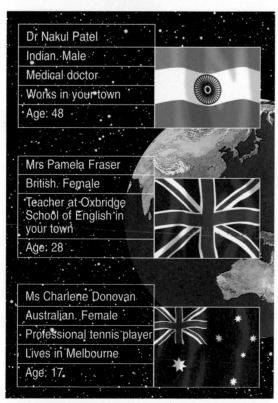

Dr Nakul Patel
Indian. Male
Medical doctor
Works in your town
Age: 48

Mrs Pamela Fraser
British. Female
Teacher at Oxbridge School of English in your town
Age: 28

Ms Charlene Donovan
Australian. Female
Professional tennis player
Lives in Melbourne
Age: 17

1 Questions

Ask and answer about the people in the boxes:

- What's (his / her) name?
- What nationality is (he / she)?
- What does (he / she) do?
- Where does (he / she) live?
- Where does (he / she) work?
- How old is (he / she)?

 See Active Grammar
present simple

2 Introducing someone

You are in your home town. How would you introduce the people in the bottom box to the people in the top box? Use these formulas.

This	is	(name)
May I Can I I'd like to	introduce	
I'd like you I want you	to meet	

Then give information about the person. What information can you give?

3 Role-play

Work in groups. Each student, in turn, chooses one person from the boxes. Go around and introduce yourself to the others. Shake hands.

19

adjectives
I think ...

Shaking hands

The 'bone crusher' handshake

The 'upper hand' handshake

The firm handshake

The limp handshake or 'dead fish'

The two-handed handshake

1 Handshakes

What kinds of handshake did you receive in the role-play on page 19?
What kind of handshake did you give?

2 First impressions

People who work with their hands (artists, musicians, surgeons etc.) often give a limp handshake. What can you tell about people from their handshakes?

She has a firm handshake.
I think she's a confident person.

Use the words opposite.

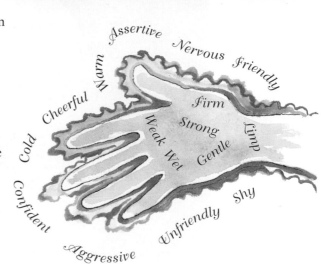

Assertive
Nervous
Friendly
Warm
Cheerful
Firm
Cold
Strong
Limp
Weak
Wet
Gentle
Confident
Shy
Unfriendly
Aggressive

Re-introducing yourself

was, were

1 Conventions

 What happens when you meet someone a long time after an introduction?
Listen to the conversations.

A: Charles! Hello!

B: Hello … uh …

A: I was at the Manchester conference last year.

B: Oh, yes … Sorry, I don't remember your name,

A: Rick Roberts … from Portway Industries.

B: Oh, yes. Nice to see you again.

A: Charles, Hello! Rick Roberts, Portway Industries? I was at the Manchester conference last year.

B: Yes, that's right. Good to see you again, Rick.

2 Questions

Who was embarrassed in the first conversation? Rick? Charles? Both of them? Was anyone embarrassed in the second conversation?

3 Role-play

These people all met at a conference in Osaka last year. Role-play a second meeting between two of them.

R·F·D INC

Paula De Souza
Chief Executive Officer

R.F.D. Inc.
210 Madison Avenue, New York, NY10016, USA

compact computers plc

Peter McFarland
SALES DIRECTOR

Maple Trading Estate, Hellesdon
Norwich, Norfolk, United Kingdom

INTERCONTINENTAL TRADING

Dorethy Cheng
West Coast Representative

2016 Parkside Avenue
Vancouver, British Columbia, Canada

Forms of address

titles
present simple
forms of
address

1 Listening

 Listen to the conversation. Tick the forms of address that they use.

The police officer uses:
..... sir / madam
..... title + first name + surname
..... title + surname
..... surname only
..... first name only
..... friendly form of first name

The driver uses:
..... sir / madam
..... job title only
..... job title + surname

Which of these are formal?

 See Active Grammar
forms of address

2 Culture comparison

Choose the correct answers for your country, then discuss them with another student.

1 In my language we have (one form / two forms) of *you*. One is formal, the other is informal.
2 I (like / don't like) the fact that English has only one form of *you*.
3 In business, we (almost never / sometimes / usually) use first names.
4 I (don't like / don't mind / prefer) it when new acquaintances use my first name.
5 My boss / head teacher calls me by (my first name / my surname only / my surname with *Mr, Ms, Mrs or Miss*).
6 Shop assistants (always / sometimes) use *Sir* and *Madam*.
7 I use *Sir* and *Madam* to (everyone that I don't know / people in superior positions / customers / older people).

3 The USA and Britain

What do you think the answers for 3 to 7 in **2** are for Britain and the USA?

Starting a conversation

was, were

1 Meeting at the airport

 What do we say after introducing ourselves? Listen to this conversation.

WOMAN Mr Costello?

MAN That's right...

WOMAN I'm Laura Miles from the London office. How do you do.

MAN Very well, thanks. Pleased to meet you, Ms Miles.

WOMAN What was your flight like?

MAN Not bad. The take-off was delayed half and hour, but we arrived on time. The plane was full, though. There wasn't an empty seat.

WOMAN Is this your first visit to England?

MAN No, I was here ten years ago. I was on vacation, not business. This is my first business trip.

WOMAN Come this way. My car's in the car park. I'll drive you to the hotel...

2 Questions

Choose the correct answers.

1 Ms Miles (knows / doesn't know) Mr Costello.
2 Mr Costello is / isn't English.
3 The take-off was (late / on time / early).
4 The arrival was (late / on time / early).
5 The plane was (full / empty).
6 This (is / isn't) Mr Costello's first visit to England.
7 Ms Miles and Mr Costello are (friends / relatives / business acquaintances / strangers).

3 Personal questions

Who asked the questions, Ms Miles or Mr Costello?
Were the questions personal?

 See Active Grammar
was, were

4 Pair work

Which is the best way to start a conversation?
Discuss these techniques with a partner.

– asking personal questions
  Are you married?
– talking about yourself
  I live near the airport. My sister works there.
– asking general questions
  What was your flight like?
– offering someone a drink / some food
  Would you like a drink before we leave the airport?

Suggest some suitable topics, and give examples of the kind of questions you can ask in this situation.

Asking questions

present
continuous

questions

going to

I'd rather (not)

1 Asking questions

We often start conversations with strangers by asking them questions. The table gives some ideas.

2 Matching

Look at the picture. Which of these questions are the people answering?

3 Interaction

Turn to the Interaction appendix.
Student A: look at section 9.
Student B: look at section 17.

Topic	Questions
Journey	What was your (flight / journey) like? How was your (flight / journey?)
Weather	What was the weather like in (England)? How was the weather in (England)?
Visits to your country	Is this your first (visit / time) here?
Food	Do you like (Italian) food? What do you think of (Italian) food?
Hotel	How's your (room / hotel)? What's your (room / hotel) like? Is everything OK at your hotel? Where are you staying?
Job	What do you do at (ABC Industries)?
Visitor's home	Which part of (England) do you come from? Where do you live in (England)?
Visitor's plans	How long are you staying here? What are you going to do (during this visit)? Why are you (here / in this country)?

4 Personal questions

Personal questions are embarrassing in different cultures. Which of these questions are embarrassing, rude, or strange in your country?

How's your family?
How old are you?
Why aren't you married?
Why haven't you got any children?
How much do you earn?
How much was your (jacket)?
How much do you weigh?
What's your star sign?
What's your blood group?
Which political party do you support?

Are there any other questions which are embarrassing in your country?

5 Avoiding the answer

Some questions are personally embarrassing as well as culturally embarrassing. Ask other students the questions opposite. If you don't want to answer, use one of these expressions:

Sorry, that's a personal question.
I don't want to answer that.
I'd rather not say / tell you / answer that.
Mind your own business!

See Active Grammar
question formation

Closing a conversation

closing
formulas

1 Closing

When you close a conversation, which of these things do you usually do?

Mention the next meeting
See you soon.
See you (at the sales conference).
I hope to see you next time (I'm here).
(I) look forward to seeing you again / soon.

Thank the person for help / a meal etc.
Thank you for all your help.
Thank you for a wonderful meal.
Thanks for everything.
It was great (seeing you / talking with you).

Give them good wishes
Have a nice day.
Have a good weekend / holiday / flight.
Enjoy the rest of your stay.
Take care (of yourself).
All the best.
Mind how you go.

2 Openings and closings

We use some expressions only for opening conversations, and others only for closing them. We can use some expressions both for opening and closing.

Write O (opening), C (closing), or O/C (opening and closing) beside each expression, as in the example.

..O. Hi!   ..... Hey!
..... See you!   ..... Goodnight.
..... Good morning. ..... Ciao!
..... Good afternoon. ..... Bye!
..... Goodbye.   ..... Hello.
..... Good evening. ..... Bye for now.

3 Goodbyes

Look at these expressions.

See you later!
Goodbye. Nice to have met you.
Goodnight. Have a good weekend.
Good evening.
Thank you for coming.
Bye!

Which of the formulas would you use for:

1 a business person you have met for the first time?
2 someone you often meet, e.g. a friend?
3 a dinner guest?
4 someone you have been speaking to for a few seconds?
5 a colleague you see when you're leaving work on Friday evening?
6 someone you are greeting after 6 p.m.?

Understanding the present

See Active Grammar

The present simple

The present continuous

1 Which is it?

Look at these sentences. Which ones are present continuous and which ones are present simple?

1 He's learning to drive.
2 I don't like coffee.
3 What does she do?
4 You aren't listening to me!
5 They live in Belfast.
6 She's wearing a green skirt.
7 Water freezes at 0°C.
8 I'm meeting her tomorrow afternoon.
9 Our flight leaves at 9 o'clock.
10 I usually finish work at 5.30.
11 He's telephoning his sister.

2 How the present is used

How do we use the present simple and the present continuous? Look at the explanations and write *PS* (present simple) or *PC* (present continuous).

1 for actions which are happening over a long period of time .....
2 for future plans .....
3 for talking about timetables .....
4 for everyday habits .....
5 for general truths, or facts .....
6 for describing people .....
7 for likes and dislikes .....
8 for actions which are happening now .....
9 for things which do not change .....

3 Present time words

Write *PC* or *PS* next to these time or frequency expressions.

1 now .....
2 usually .....
3 every day .....
4 this week .....
5 once a week .....
6 at the moment .....
7 often .....
8 on Monday mornings .....

4 Structure – the present continuous

Complete the sentences.

1 She ..... studying English at school.
2 They ..... visiting Glasgow on business.
3 I ..... watching TV.
4 ..... you enjoying the programme?
5 No, he ..... working at the moment.
6 ..... it raining?
7 No, they ..... staying at the hotel.

5 Structure – the present simple

Choose the correct verb.

1 He (doesn't / don't) like football.
2 I (have / has) a bath every morning.
3 Our bus (leave / leaves) at 8.30.
4 What does he (do / does)?
5 Jumbo jets (fly / flies) at 11,000 metres.
6 I (doesn't / don't) understand.
7 She (works /work) for IBM.

6 Continuous or simple?

Marcel Canona is a famous footballer. He plays for Melchester United. At the moment, Marcel is standing in a street in Melchester, and he's signing autographs for his fans.

Look at this:

What does Marcel do?
He plays football for Melchester United / He's a footballer.

What's Marcel doing?
He's signing autographs.

Write two questions for each of these situations. Answer them.

Philip and Maria work at NatWest Bank in Blackpool. They're bank clerks. They're sitting in Maria's car at the moment and they're listening to the radio.

Shelley's a computer programmer. She lives in Seattle. She's on holiday in Europe at the moment and she's visiting the Eiffel Tower today.

Using the present

1 Actions over a long period of time

Which of these things are you doing at the moment? Ask a partner:

Are you reading a good book at the moment?
No, I'm not. / Yes, I am. I'm reading 'Lord of the Rings'.

– reading a good book
– learning a foreign language
– saving money to buy something
– revising for an exam
– living away from your home town
– making or building something

2 Regular habits

Which of these things do you do regularly? Ask a partner:

Do you take exercise?
No, I don't. / Yes, I do. I play tennis.

– take exercise
– read a newspaper
– listen to music in a car
– put money in a bank or savings account
– write letters to friends
– watch TV at breakfast time
– listen to the radio

3 How often do you do things?

Look back at **2**. Ask and answer:

How often do you play tennis?
I never play tennis / Twice a week / I play tennis every Saturday, etc.

4 Describing people and actions

Work with a partner. Close your eyes. Describe your partner's clothes. Describe other people in the room. Say where they are sitting and what they are doing.

5 Likes and dislikes

Write a list of four things that you like and four things that you don't like. Interview a partner. Ask questions and guess what is on their list.

Do you like opera?
Yes, I do / No, I don't.

Change partners. Ask about the previous partner's list.

Does (she) like (rap music)?
Yes, she does / No, she doesn't.

6 Matching

Find the best words in column B to complete the sentences in column A.

Column A

1 'Why are you here?' 'I'm visiting …'
2 I visit this town …
3 I'm reading 'War & Peace' …
4 I read …
5 I'm learning …
6 I study English …
7 I'm having …
8 I have …
9 I'm meeting my sister …
10 I often meet …

Column B

a lot of crime novels A
three times a week B
twice a year C
problems at work D
a shower every morning E
tomorrow evening F
foreign visitors G
on business H
to drive I
at the moment J

Gesture

1 Matching

What do their gestures mean? Match the sentences to the pictures.

A It wasn't me! I didn't do anything!
B Don't do that again!
C The bill, please.
D I don't know.
E Be quiet!

2 An international language?

Do other students agree with your choices? Do you think these gestures mean the same in every country?

In Bulgaria, nodding the head means 'no'. Almost everywhere else, shaking the head means 'no'.

3 What gestures?

Can you use gestures to express these things?
– Come here.   – Go away.
– I'd like a drink.   – You're crazy!
– That's perfect.   – It's over there.
– Keep calm.   – This is boring.
– OK?   – Who? Me?

Are there any other gestures which you often use? Demonstrate them.

4 Role-play

Work in pairs. Student A is a tourist. Student B is a waiter. Neither of them can speak any of the other's language. Use gesture and mime to communicate.

Student A arrives, gets a table, orders spaghetti and a drink, and finally pays without saying anything. The waiter can speak, but the customer doesn't understand.

UNIT TWO

Dress and appearance

adjectives

present
continuous

frequency
adverbs

| sweater | tie | scarf | earrings | bracelet | necklace | blouse | jeans | jewellery | wig |

1 Personal appearance

Describe the people in the pictures.
- What does (she) look like?
- How old is (he)?

general:	attractive, casual, well-dressed, scruffy, smart *She is (attractive) / She looks (smart)*
face:	a beard, a moustache, glasses *He has (got) (a beard) / She's wearing (glasses)*
hair:	long, blonde, short, dark, wavy, bald *His hair is (long) / He has (got) (long) hair / He is (bald)*
build:	(quite) tall, overweight, short, medium-height, slim, average build *She is (slim)*
age:	middle-aged, about 45, in her twenties *They are (in their fifties)*

2 Describing clothes

Describe the clothes they are wearing.
- What's (she) wearing?
- What colour's (his shirt)?

3 Giving the right impression

Our first impression of people comes from their appearance. Look at the words below and write F for *formal* appearance, C for *casual* appearance.

..... loose clothes   ..... beards
..... tailored clothes   ..... bare legs
..... clean-shaven faces   ..... light colours
..... matt leather shoes   ..... dark colours
..... long, loose hair   ..... styled hair
..... polished shoes   ..... red lipstick

| hat | gown | trousers | skirt | dress | uniform | two-piece suit | open-necked shirt | three-piece suit |

4 Guessing

Make guesses about the people.

I think he's Australian / a rock star / in his forties.

Give reasons.

Why do you think he's a rock star?
Because he's wearing jeans and he has got long hair.

5 Do you recognize them?

 Sometimes appearances can give the wrong impression.

Turn to the Interaction appendix.
Student A: look at section 34.
Student B: look at section 28.

6 Image and appearance

Do you agree with these statements?
- I think formal clothes give you authority.
- A casual appearance is more relaxed and friendly.
- I feel more comfortable when I'm wearing similar clothes to people around me.
- I like to be different.

7 At work

In some companies employees can wear jeans on Friday. Is this a good idea?
Are there formal rules about clothes / hair style in your country?
Do men usually wear suits and ties?
Do women often wear trousers at work?
Are habits changing? How?

◆ **See Active Grammar**
frequency adverbs

Body Language

look, feel etc.
imperatives
adjectives with
-ed

1   Can you read body language?

Look at these pictures and answer the questions.

1   Tick the words which describe this person:
   ☐ sincere   ☐ shy   ☐ relaxed
   ☐ confident   ☐ nervous   ☐ honest

2   Does she look:
   a. angry?   c. bored?
   b. embarrassed?   d. interested?

   Can he read her body language?

3   Do they like each other?

4   Does he look friendly and co-operative,
    or does he look unfriendly and
    unco-operative?

5 Which one is the boss?

6 Does she look interested or bored?

2 How do you feel?

Follow these instructions.

> Lean back in your chair. Cross your legs. Fold your arms. Look down.

Do you feel in a bad mood?
This is negative body language.

> Lean forward in your chair. Put both feet on the ground, about 30 cm apart. Put your hands loosely together. Look straight ahead. Smile.

Do you feel in a good mood?
This is positive body language.

> Stand up. Put your legs apart. Put your hands on your hips. Look straight ahead. Don't smile.

Do you want a fight?
This is aggressive body language.

3 Observation

Two students come to the front of the class. Student A reads out the questions below, imagining that this is an oral test in English. Student B replies. The rest of the class observes the body language.
- You look nervous. Are you feeling nervous?
- Do you like speaking English in front of the class?
- How often do you practise your English at home?
- Are you telling the truth?
- I think your English is excellent. Do you agree?
- Do you like the other people in your class?
- Do they like you?
- Describe your personality. What kind of person are you?
- Describe me. What kind of person am I?
- Would you like to ask me the questions now?

4 Task

Ask and answer the questions above in pairs three times.
First, stand with your hands at your sides, and your head still.
Next, stand still, but move your head and eyes.
Finally, relax. You can move as much as you like.

5 Project

Look back at picture 3. They are enjoying their conversation. We know this because they are copying each other's body language. This is called mirroring. We don't usually know that we are doing this, it just happens. If you mirror someone's body language, they usually feel that you are sympathetic.

Try this with a conversation in your own language after the class (but not with students from your class!).

 See Active Grammar
adjectives; *look* + adjective

adjectives
look etc.
frequency
adverbs

Facial expression

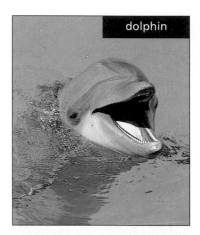 dolphin

 wolf

 dog

 gorilla

 mouse

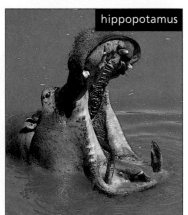 hippopotamus

1 Animal faces

We don't know how animals are feeling, but we often think we do!

Make sentences about the animals. You can use words from the list below.

The dolphin looks happy.

happy	worried	tired
surprised	scared	wise
serious	depressed	bored
sad	angry	nervous

2 What's she like?

Describe people in your class.

She always looks cheerful.
He never smiles.
She often looks sad.
He's hardly ever nervous.

Your partner guesses who you are describing.

3 Parts of the face

chin	mouth	teeth	lips
cheek	ear	nose	nostril
eye	eyelid	eyebrow	forehead

Look at the words above. Work with a partner and identify them.

Student A demonstrates:
smiling / yawning / frowning / crying / thinking
Student B notes which parts of the face are moving.

 See Active Grammar
frequency adverbs

Making the right noises

noises

can

going to

agreeing

1 Listening

 Listen to these five conversations. You're going to hear the English sounds in the picture.

Match the sounds with the meanings below.

A Isn't that cute (USA) / sweet (UK)?
B Now I understand!
C Give me time to think.
D I'm listening.
E Excuse me? (USA) / Pardon? (UK)

2 Compare your language

What sounds do you use to express these meanings in your language?

3 Misunderstandings

 A client is trying to do a deal with a bank. Her company wants a loan. Listen to the bank director's reactions, and write them in the blanks.

CLIENT My company needs forty million dollars for the new project.
BANK DIRECTOR ....
CLIENT We're going to build a new office in Singapore.
BANK DIRECTOR ....
CLIENT We can pay back the money – there's no problem with that.
BANK DIRECTOR ....
CLIENT I can have my accountants call you next week.
BANK DIRECTOR ....
CLIENT So, we have a deal ...
BANK DIRECTOR ....

1 Does the bank director react with affirmatives?
2 Does he mean 'yes, I agree' or does he mean 'yes, I'm listening to you'?
3 How can you tell?
4 What does she think that he means?
5 Is *we have a deal* a question or a statement?

4 Non-committal sounds

Listen to conversation 2. This time the bank director's reactions are different.

1 In this conversation, does *Uh-huh* mean 'I agree' or 'I'm listening to you'?
2 How can you tell?
3 Does she understand what he means?
4 Is *we have a deal* a question or a statement?

5 Agreeing?

Role-play the conversation with a partner. First, the bank director is very enthusiastic and wants to lend the money. Say *Yes / OK / Right* with enthusiasm.

Second, the bank director is non-committal. The bank director speaks with flat intonation.

Third, role-play the bank director and try to express other feelings with *Uh-huh* – surprise, disbelief etc.

Fourth, the bank director is absolutely silent, but expresses himself with body language and facial expressions.

Eye contact

prepositions of place

adverbs of movement

1 It's all in the eyes

Which of the words below describe the people in the pictures?

You can use a dictionary. Compare with other students.

shifty	confident	cold	hard
shy	dishonest	sly	modest
strong	determined	sexy	aggressive

Which of these adjectives have a positive meaning, and which have a negative meaning?

2 Definitions

Match the expressions with the definitions.

Expression

1 to see eye to eye with somebody
2 to look up to someone
3 to look down on someone
4 to look someone up and down
5 to look someone straight in the eye

Definition

to be honest with someone A
to respect, admire someone B
to agree with someone C
to feel that you are superior to someone; D
that someone is inferior to you
to inspect someone; to judge someone E
by their appearance

3 Compare your language

Are there any expressions in your language like these? Translate them into English.

4 Reading aloud

Work in groups of three. Practise reading a text aloud. Try to use eye contact. Turn to the Interaction appendix.
Student A: look at section 23.
Student B: look at section 31.
Student C: look at section 8.

5 Speakers and listeners

The class is going to observe some conversations in pairs. In each, one person will do most of the speaking and the other person will be mainly listening.
Choose three students as speakers.
Speakers: you are going to talk about a topic for about 30 seconds. Choose a topic (possible topics: your hobby, breakfast, your family).
Listeners: turn to the Interaction appendix, section 5.
Each speaker works with a listener while the class observes. What did you notice about each interaction? Discuss.

6 What about your country?

In your country:
– Is it rude to stare at strangers?
– Do sales people use a lot of eye contact?
– Do men wink at women?
– Do employees avoid eye contact with their bosses?

 See Active Grammar
prepositions of place; adverbs of movement; seeing verbs

location:
prepositions /
adverbs

Position

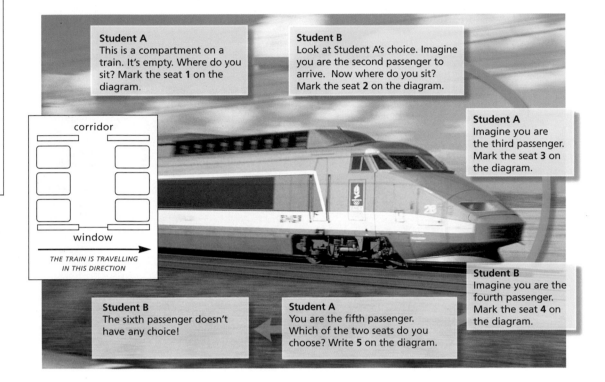

Student A
This is a compartment on a train. It's empty. Where do you sit? Mark the seat **1** on the diagram.

Student B
Look at Student A's choice. Imagine you are the second passenger to arrive. Now where do you sit? Mark the seat **2** on the diagram.

corridor

window

THE TRAIN IS TRAVELLING
IN THIS DIRECTION

Student A
Imagine you are the third passenger. Mark the seat **3** on the diagram.

Student B
Imagine you are the fourth passenger. Mark the seat **4** on the diagram.

Student B
The sixth passenger doesn't have any choice!

Student A
You are the fifth passenger. Which of the two seats do you choose? Write **5** on the diagram.

at the other end of the row nearest / furthest away from (ie. window) with your back to the engine	next to / beside in the middle opposite	on the same side on the other side facing the engine

1 A compartment on a train

Pairwork. Look at the picture and follow the instructions. Imagine you are complete strangers on a train.

2 Class survey

Use the words above, and discuss your choices with the class. Analyse the choices.

First choice:
How many people chose a seat:
– next to the window?
– with your back to the engine?

Second choice:
How many people chose the seat:
– opposite the first passenger?
– beside the first passenger?
– furthest away on the same side?
– furthest away on the other side?

Continue with the remaining choices.

3 Travelling habits

When you get on a train, bus or plane, where do you put your newspaper/ bag / coat?
Do you put them on the seat beside you / on your lap / in the baggage rack?

Does this depend on whether…
– it's empty?
– it's full?
– more people are going to get on?

Do you prefer to have an empty seat next to you?
How can you try to keep it empty?
Do you prefer to have someone to talk to?

Do you have a story about a travelling experience? Share it with the class.

 See Active Grammar
location

Proximity

too / very

comparison

*each other /
one another*

1 Reading

Keep your distance

Police officers in all societies always stand very close to people when they are interrogating them, and managers often stand close when they are trying to get information from their staff. Teachers sometimes do this with students, too! We all feel uncomfortable when someone stands or sits too close to us. We think of the space near our bodies as our territory. But what is 'too close'?

All over the world, people in big cities stand closer to one another than people in small towns, and people in small towns stand closer to one another than people from the country. The idea of personal space changes in different countries. In some parts of India people stay 60 cm apart. In Britain, Australia and North America personal space for most people is about 45 cm from the body. Researchers say it is 25 cm in Japan but only 20 cm in both Denmark and Brazil.

This difference can cause communication problems. Latin Americans and Asians often say that the British and Americans are cold and unfriendly. On the other hand, the British and Americans often see other cultures as too assertive and aggressive. In both examples, the problems are different ideas of personal space.

2 True or false?

Are these statements about the text true (✓) or false (✗)?

1 Police officers stand close when they're asking questions. .....
2 We don't like it when people stand too close. .....
3 People in small towns stand closer than people in cities. .....
4 People in the country stand further apart than people in small towns. .....

5 North Americans like a larger personal space than Danish people. .....
6 Brazilians stand closer to people than the Japanese. .....
7 The British and Americans are very cold. .....
8 The British and Americans like more personal space. .....

  See Active Grammar
too / very; comparison; *each other / one another*

Touching

vocabulary
development

dictionary skills

cultural
awareness

1 Touching words

Look at these definitions:

> **pat** /ˈpæt/ *verb* touch or tap someone repeatedly in a gentle way with the open hand
>
> **stroke** /ˈstrəʊk/ *verb* move the hand gently backwards and forwards repeatedly
>
> **smack** /ˈsmæk/ *verb* hit someone (usually a child) with an open hand
>
> **slap** /ˈslæp/ *verb* hit someone with an open hand
>
> **punch** /ˈpʌnʧ/ *verb* hit someone hard with the fist (closed hand)
>
> **nudge** /ˈnʌʤ/ *verb* touch or push with the elbow because you want to get someone's attention
>
> **pinch** /ˈpɪnʧ/ *verb* squeeze tightly between the thumb and forefinger
>
> **tickle** /ˈtɪkl/ *verb* touch the skin (especially in sensitive areas) very lightly in order to make someone laugh
>
> **cuddle** /ˈkʌdl/ *verb* hold someone close and lovingly in your arms
>
> **hug** /ˈhʌg/ *verb* put the arms tightly around someone

Do you think the sound of the word helps you to remember its meaning? Note that these words can also be nouns.

2 Crossword

Work with a partner and complete this crossword. Remember third person endings and past tenses!

3 Questionnaire

What happens in your country? Complete this questionnaire.

> 1 When men shake hands, do they touch any other part of the body?
>
> ☐ they touch the arm
> ☐ they touch the shoulder
> ☐ they pat the back
> ☐ none of the above

> 2 Do acquaintances touch each other when they're talking?
>
> ☐ never ☐ sometimes ☐ always
> ☐ hardly ever ☐ often

> 3 Where do they touch each other?
>
> ☐ nowhere
> ☐ on the hand
> ☐ on the arm
> ☐ on the shoulder
> ☐ an arm around the back
> ☐ on the head

> 4 You are crossing a busy road with an acquaintance (not a child or an elderly person). Do you touch them?
>
> ☐ no
> ☐ I hold their arm
> ☐ I hold their hand
> ☐ we link our arms

CLUES

Across

1 In a boxing match one boxer ..... (7) the other.
5 My son hates it when his grandfather ..... (4) him on the head.
7 Don't ..... (6) me! It makes me laugh too much.

Down

2 The American President gave the Russian President a ..... (3) at the airport.
3 I don't think parents should ..... (5) their children.
4 He isn't listening to the lecture! ..... (5) him and wake him up!
5 Mary ..... (7) her brother on the arm and made him cry.
6 Nurses sometimes ..... (6) patients' hands when they're ill.
8 You ..... (6) people that you love.
9 If he says that again, I'll ..... (4) him across the face!

comparison

prefer

I'd rather

Status symbols

1 Status symbols

Which of these things are status symbols in your country?
How many of them can you find in the picture?

job title	foreign travel	being near a window	keys to the executive washroom
qualifications	health insurance	type of computer	business / first class travel tickets
holidays	company car	size of desk	
size of office	club membership	gold credit cards	
private office	office furniture		

2 Status symbols at work

Are you interested in status? Which of these things would you prefer to have in a work situation?
– a larger office or a quieter office?
– a larger chair or a more comfortable chair?
– a more powerful computer or a bigger desk?
– more money or a better job title?
– a newer car or a more powerful car?
– longer holidays or a shorter working week?

Make sentences.

I'd prefer more money / I'd prefer to have more money.
I'd rather have more money.

3 Discuss

Look at the status symbols and discuss them in groups. Decide:
– Which ones are most important in your company / country?
– Which ones are most important to you?
– Which ones are least important to you?
– Which status symbols would you like to have? Why?
– Do you think men and women have different status symbols? Can you give examples?
– What status symbols do teenagers have?

 See Active Grammar
comparison

Adjectives

See Active Grammar

adjectives

look + adjective

determiners

possessive adjectives

1 What are the rules?

Compare English with your language. Look at the rules about English adjectives. Does your language have the same rules (write *S*) or different rules (write *D*)?

1 Adjectives don't have singular and plural forms:
an old book, some old books, Italian rice, Italian tomatoes, an Italian lemon. .....

2 Adjectives don't agree with person:
She's an interesting woman. He's an interesting man. They're interesting people. .....

3 Adjectives go before nouns:
some casual shoes, a formal dress. .....

4 Numbers / articles come before adjectives:
an old book, five blue pens, a lot of new students, a few difficult questions. .....

Is the grammar of adjectives simpler in your language or in English?

2 Adjectives and articles

We use *an* before the sound of a vowel. Write *a* or *an* in the spaces.

1 ..... empty seat
2 ..... wrong impression
3 ..... new employee
4 ..... American client
5 ..... interesting idea
6 ..... unfriendly look
7 ..... casual appearance
8 ..... anxious face

3 Possessive adjectives

Complete the spaces.

subject pronoun	object pronoun	possessive adjective	possessive pronoun
I	me	my	mine
you	you	.....	yours
he	him	.....	his
she	her	.....	hers
it	it	.....	—
we	us	.....	ours
they	them	.....	theirs

4 Parts of the body

Write a list of parts of the body, e.g. *foot, knee, shoulder.*

Add *-ed* to the nouns on your list. Be careful! You may have to double some consonants, e.g. *leg / legged, chin / chinned.*

You now have a list of past participles. Some of them can be used as verbs, others can be used as adjectives. Underline the ones used as adjectives in the text.

> Charmaine's a long-legged, dark-haired, blue-eyed super-model. Gary's a warm-hearted, square-jawed, left-footed international striker. They were in a night club. Charmaine saw Gary and eyed him up and down. Gary shouldered his way through the crowd. He was wearing an open-necked shirt and a double-breasted jacket. Charmaine was wearing a low-backed dress and high-heeled shoes. Gary gave her a gap-toothed smile, handed her a flower and asked her to dance. She wasn't a very good dancer and accidentally kneed Gary in the leg. He backed into a table, open-mouthed with surprise. Gary couldn't play the next Saturday and no one believed the reason for his accident.

5 Adjective order

When there are two adjectives, opinions (*lovely, nice, boring*) come before facts (*old, plastic, square*).

a lovely new dress
an interesting old story

Put these words in the correct order, and add *a, an,* or *some.*

1 car / Italian / beautiful
2 exciting / movie / action
3 beard / untidy / brown
4 shoes / leather / smart
5 aggressive / salespeople / young
6 cotton / nice / trousers

Adverbs

See Active Grammar

adverbs of manner

frequency adverbs

1 Adjectives and adverbs

Are the words in bold adjectives (write *ADJ*) or adverbs (write *ADV*)?

1 Their answers were **wrong**. .....
2 She plays tennis **well**. .....
3 He looked **unhappy**. .....
4 They looked **carefully** before they crossed the street. .....
5 I **sometimes** get up at 7 o'clock. .....
6 The music was very **loud**. .....
7 It's a **fast** motor cycle. .....
8 The car is travelling **fast**. .....

Look back at the nine questions. Which words do the adjectives and adverbs describe? What part of speech are the words?

answers – noun   *plays* – verb

2 What's the adverb?

Look at the list of adjectives below. Write the adverb next to the adjective.

slow *slowly*   fast *fast*

honest .....   good .....   polite .....
bad .....   hard .....   careless .....
quiet .....   weak .....   firm .....

3 Using adverbs

Ask a partner these questions.

1 Do you speak English slowly?
2 Do English people speak quickly?
3 Do you stop when you make a mistake?
4 Do you move your hands frequently when you're talking?
5 Do you sit still when you're listening?
6 Do you look at people carefully when you're listening to them?

4 Frequency adverbs

Frequency adverbs tell us how often something happens or happened. Time expressions tell us when something is happening or happened.

Underline the frequency expressions.

always	every day	yesterday
nearly always	sometimes	often
almost never	twice a day	then
three times a week	generally	normally
at the moment	last night	never
two weeks ago	hardly ever	now
every two hours	at 6 o'clock	usually

5 Word order

Frequency adverbs normally go before the main verb (*take, work, seen*), but after auxiliary verbs (*don't, 've*).

I often take work home.
I don't usually work on Saturdays.
I've never seen the Queen.

Frequency adverbs come after the verb *to be*.

I'm rarely late for work.
We were often late for school.

Put the frequency adverbs into these sentences.

1 I watch TV in the evenings. (always)
2 I kiss friends when we meet. (never)
3 I'm tired in the mornings. (rarely)
4 She goes to work by train. (generally)
5 In London, temperatures are below 0°C in March. (hardly ever)
6 The flight arrives at eleven. (normally)

6 How often ...? / Do you ever ...?

Ask a partner about the things below.

listen to the radio

Q: *How often do you listen to the radio?*
   Do you ever listen to the radio?

A: *I hardly ever listen to the radio.*
   I sometimes listen to the radio in the car.
   I always listen to the radio in the morning.

eat in restaurants / go to sleep after midnight / meet foreigners / watch sport on TV / take exercise / drink coffee with breakfast / travel abroad / study English at home

Personal information

personal details

question
formation

1 Matching

Match the captions with the pictures.
Then check with your partner.

Captions
A 43. Albert Einstein was born in: (a) Colorado Springs (b) Ulm (c) Zurich. 44. H_2SO_4 is …
B Albert and Gertrude Butcher with their family in 1887
C Mr Bun works in a bakery.
D She graduated from Bradford University with a B.Sc. in Physics.
E Brian's birthday – 21 today
F Konishiki weighs 253.3 kilograms.
G Name, Roderick, initials, T.J. Rank, Captain. Number 4593218760
H … I'm single, I have blue eyes and blonde hair. I like wind-surfing, and my telephone number is…

2   3

4   5

6

7   8

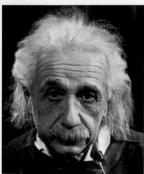

Mr. Bun the Baker

2 Facts about yourself

Write five facts about yourself. Tell them to
your partner. Keep your list of facts – you will
need them again at the end of this unit!

Walk to the front of the class and present your
five facts.

Find out more information about your
partner. Ask your partner five questions.

In groups: write five questions that you want
to ask your teacher about himself / herself.
Ask them.

See Active Grammar
question formation

Origins

was, were
past simple
families

1 Social conversation

 Listen to the conversations with books closed. Then listen and read.

Answer the questions about Rosalita.

1 Where are her parents from?
2 Where did they get married?
3 When did they move to Texas?
4 Where was she born?
5 Why did they move to Los Angeles?
6 How old was she then?
7 Where did she grow up?

Here are the answers to some questions about Hamish. Ask the questions.

8 Scotland.
9 Ireland.
10 England.
11 London.
12 Westminster.
13 Liverpool.

HAMISH Rosalita? That's a nice name. Is it Spanish?
ROSALITA Yes. My parents are Mexican.
HAMISH Really?
ROSALITA They're from Tampico. They got married there, but they moved to Texas before I was born.
HAMISH Where were you born?
ROSALITA I was born in Houston. Then my father got a job with General Motors and we moved to Los Angeles when I was about a year old. So I grew up in California.

(pause)

ROSALITA Your name's Scottish, isn't it?
HAMISH Yes, it is. My father's Scottish and my mother's Irish. She comes from Dublin. My parents met in England.
ROSALITA So, where were you born, Hamish?
HAMISH London. I went to school in Westminster. Then I went to university in Liverpool. And at the moment I'm looking for a job.

2 Pair work

Ask your partner about their past.

3 Family history

Choose some relatives and write some sentences about them.

Tell the class.

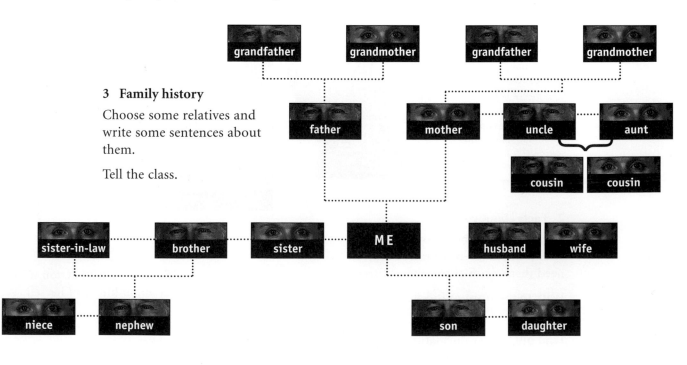

present simple
past simple
can (ability)
-ing forms

Your life and skills

1 Help your partner to compose a résumé

A résumé or curriculum vitae (CV) is a summary of your life and your skills.
You usually prepare one when you are looking for a job. Work together,
answering the questions in the boxes. Write your résumés on separate pieces
of paper. Keep your résumé; you will need it later in this unit.

curriculum vitae

Personal details

name
address
telephone number

(and in some countries, date of birth, sex, and marital status)

Note: In the USA, employers cannot ask about your age, sex, race, or marital status.

Work experience

What is / was your job / job title?
Where do / did you work?
When did you work there? (... from ... to ...)
What do / did you do in your job?

Are you going to begin the list with your first job, or your most recent job?

Personal qualities

Which of these things are you good at doing?
– communicating with people
– using machines
– working with your hands
– selling things
– thinking of new ideas
– organizing yourself / other people / information
– working by yourself / in a team
– learning languages

Special skills / interests

Do you have any special skills or training?
(e.g.word processing / first aid / sports)
Do you do any voluntary work or community service?
Do you have any certificates?
Where did you get them?
(e.g. during military service, at an evening class)
Can you drive?
Can you play a musical instrument?
Do you have any hobbies?
What do you like doing in your free time?

Education

What qualifications do you have?
What subjects are you studying?
Which schools / colleges did you attend / are you attending?
When were you there?

Are you going to begin with your earliest qualification, your most recent qualification or your most important qualification?

Languages

Which languages can you speak?
What level are you (elementary / intermediate / fluent)?

List any certificates you have.

2 Sentences about yourself

Make sentences about yourself with:
I'm very good / good / quite good / not very good at …
I enjoy / don't enjoy …

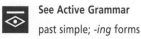

See Active Grammar
past simple; *-ing* forms

Checking information

questions
question tags

1 Checking information on the phone

 Victoria is calling Computer Line, a mail order software company.

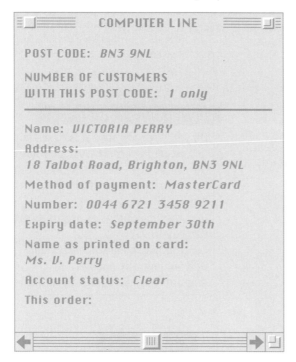

COMPUTER LINE

POST CODE: *BN3 9NL*

NUMBER OF CUSTOMERS
WITH THIS POST CODE: *1 only*

Name: *VICTORIA PERRY*

Address:
18 Talbot Road, Brighton, BN3 9NL

Method of payment: *MasterCard*

Number: *0044 6721 3458 9211*

Expiry date: *September 30th*

Name as printed on card:
Ms. V. Perry

Account status: *Clear*

This order:

Listen to the recording.
Which facts does Alan check?
How does he check them? (What does he say?)
Can you copy his intonation?

2 Question tags

One way of checking information is to use question tags. Listen to the example. The speaker is checking the facts on a résumé and is expecting confirmation.

Q: *You live in London, don't you?*
A: *Yes, I do.*
Q: *You don't have a job at the moment, do you?*
A: *No, I don't.*

Now ask and answer the following questions.

1 You can drive, can't you?
2 You can't speak French, can you?
3 You went to university, didn't you?
4 You didn't go to graduate school, did you?
5 You've been to the USA, haven't you?
6 You haven't been to France, have you?
7 You were in the army, weren't you?
8 You weren't in any sports teams, were you?

3 Pair work

Exchange résumés with a partner. Choose five or six facts on your partner's résumé, and check them. Look at the pictures below, and observe your partner's body language.

See Active Grammar
question tags

When interviewers check information they need to understand body language.

Showing the palms
'I'm telling the truth!' (whether he is or not)

Looking from side to side
'There's something I don't want to tell you.'

Hand on chin
'I don't believe what I'm saying.'

Touching the nose
'I'm telling a lie'

Saying the wrong thing

present perfect
ever
how long?
adjectives

1 Before you listen

Ms Driscoll is the Personnel Manager of a large hotel group, and she is going to interview applicants for a job as a reception clerk. What kind of person is she looking for? Look at the list below and choose the five most important personal qualities:

- ☐ polite
- ☐ friendly
- ☐ confident
- ☐ patient
- ☐ ambitious
- ☐ enthusiastic
- ☐ punctual
- ☐ nice voice

- ☐ pleasant appearance
- ☐ interested in people
- ☐ sincere
- ☐ reliable
- ☐ co-operative
- ☐ loyal to the company
- ☐ sense of humour
- ☐ honest

Make sentences.

She's looking for someone who is reliable.
She's looking for someone who has a sense of humour.

2 Listening

 These are the notes that Ms Driscoll made about seven different applicants. You are going to hear extracts from the seven interviews. Write the number of the interview next to the appropriate note.

Replies were too short. Didn't give enough information.

Replies were not clear. Difficult to understand. Poor communication.

Too many personal problems!

Replies were too long, and the information was not relevant – it was off the point.

Only interested in the money and the holidays!

Criticized previous employers – not very loyal.

Knows nothing about the job. Not interested.

3 Listen again

Listen again. Pause after each interview and list the questions that Ms Driscoll asked. Check your list with the transcript in the Listening appendix.

4 Experience of work and travel

Ask a partner these questions. Keep your answers short and to the point.

Yes, I have. / No, I haven't. / Five years. / Canada.

- How many jobs have you had / schools have you been to?
- How long have you had your present job / been at your present school?
- How many job interviews have you had?
- Have you ever worked in a (hotel)?
- Have you ever used your English at work?
- Have you ever been abroad?
- Have you ever been to an English-speaking country?

See Active Grammar
present perfect

Receiving information

pronunciation
spelling
clarification

1 Telephone messages

When you answer a phone for someone else, do you offer to take a message?

If you take a message, do you write it down?

If you write it down, do you check spelling and numbers?

2 Test your memory

Look at the three boxes for 30 seconds. Then close the book and write down what was in them.

A unique collection of complicated memory activities

432881096377

G Y B V W W B Y G V

Which was the most difficult to remember?

3 Whispers

Try this simple test. Write down a sequence of ten letters and numbers. You can mix them up in any way that you want.

Work in groups. During this activity say things once only – do not repeat them! Whisper your sequence to another student, who whispers it to another student and so on. The last student then says the sequence aloud. Did an accurate message get through?

4 Air Traffic Control

Air traffic controllers have to note numbers and letters accurately. When they're saying the numbers 5 and 9, they say *five* and *niner* because *five* and *nine* can sound similar over a radio. They say *one four* and *four zero* because *14* and *40* sound similar. They also use an international list of words instead of letters. The aircraft registration G-ATBC becomes *Golf Alpha Tango Bravo Charlie*. The police use the same system.

A	Alpha	N	November
B	Bravo	O	Oscar
C	Charlie	P	Papa
D	Delta	Q	Quebec
E	Echo	R	Romeo
F	Foxtrot	S	Sierra
G	Golf	T	Tango
H	Hotel	U	Uniform
I	India	V	Victor
J	Juliet	W	Whisky
K	Kilo	X	X-ray
L	Lima	Y	Yankee
M	Mike	Z	Zulu

Does your country have a different list for use within the country?

Did you know that ...?

- Half of the world's international business telephone calls are in English.

- Nine out of ten phone messages are either wrong, or create the need for another call (to find out what the first call was about).

- Replying to phone messages can account for 40% of a company's phone bill.

- About 50% of business calls do not reach the right person.

5 Pair work

Work with a partner. Design your own list of English words from A to Z. Remember to avoid using two words which sound very similar. Here are some groups of words you can think about:

cities / countries / composers / first names / fruit and vegetables / international words (e.g. pizza, sandwich, jet)

6 Spell it out

 Listen, and practise the dialogues.

OPERATOR Book Megastores.
CALLER Can I speak to Ms Linden, please?
OPERATOR Certainly. Who shall I say is calling?
CALLER Andy Gascoigne.
OPERATOR Sorry, can you spell that?
CALLER Yes, that's G for grammar, A for adjective, S for singular …

Now practise using these surnames. They are on the recording. Use your list from 5.

FITZGERALD   WAVERLEY
BUCKMASTER   QUARTERJACK
KNIGHT   POZZO

7 Taking a message

When you take a message on the telephone, which of these pieces of information do you note?

- date of call
- time of call
- the caller's name
- the caller's company name
- the caller's telephone number
- the reason for the call
- a convenient time for someone to return the call
- a message

Listen to this telephone call and note the message. Then read the message to your partner.

8 Interaction

You are going to role-play two telephone conversations. Turn to the Interaction appendix.
Student A: look at section 6.
Student B: look at section 13.

After you have finished the role-plays, compare your notes with your partner.

Question types

reading

yes / no questions

wh- questions

1 Reading

Read the text below.

The First TV Politician

Nowadays politicians in all countries use television during elections. TV is an important part of any modern democracy. The first time that TV showed its power was during the 1960 Presidential election in the United States. The candidates were Vice-President Richard Nixon (Republican) and Senator John F. Kennedy (Democrat). The two candidates agreed to a series of four television debates. By 1960, 88% of American homes had a TV. Historians believe that the TV debates won the election for Kennedy.

The first debate was on September 26th 1960 at 8.30 pm Chicago Time. Nixon looked awful. He had dark facial hair and always looked unshaven. He tried to cover this with a cosmetic called 'Lazy Shave'. It wasn't a professional TV cosmetic, and it began to melt under the hot studio lights. Nixon also had sweat all over his face, and dark areas under his eyes because he had been ill in hospital two weeks earlier. He was wearing a light grey suit.

By contrast, Kennedy looked young and also serious. He wore a dark suit, and was very careful about body language. He didn't use many gestures. He spoke directly to the camera (and therefore to the TV audience) when he was talking to Nixon.

Nixon looked at Kennedy while he was speaking to him, not at the camera. When Kennedy asked a question, Nixon moved his eyes from side to side. He looked dishonest. The TV audience of 70 million people thought that Kennedy won the debate.

The debate was also broadcast to a large radio audience. Some surveys showed that the radio audience thought that the two candidates were equal in the debate. Other surveys showed a small majority of radio listeners thought Nixon had won the debate! When Nixon later won the 1968 and 1972 elections, he had a large team of media advisers.

2 Question practice

Paragraph 1:

Answer these questions with *Yes* or *No*.

1 Was there a Presidential election in 1960?
2 Was Kennedy a Republican?
3 Was Nixon a Democrat?
4 Did Kennedy win?

Answer these questions with one-word replies.

5 What percentage of homes had a TV in 1960?
6 Who was Vice-President of the United States in 1960?
7 How many debates did they agree to?
8 Who won the 1960 election?

Paragraph 2:

Answer the first question, then ask another question beginning with the word in brackets.

1 Was the first debate in October? (When?)
2 Did Nixon look unshaven? (Why?)
3 Did the cosmetic melt? (Why?)
4 Was he wearing jeans? (What?)

See Active Grammar
question types

Paragraph 3:

1 Why did Kennedy look serious?
2 Why didn't Kennedy look at Nixon while he was talking?
3 Why did Nixon have poor eye contact with the TV audience?
4 Why did Nixon look dishonest?
5 How did Kennedy make a better impression on TV?

Paragraph 4:

1 Did Nixon speak well? How do you know?
2 What advice do you think Nixon received in 1968?

3 Think about these questions

Is it fair to judge people by their appearance? Which do you think is more important, the things you say or how you say them? Why is it important for politicians to have a good TV personality?

4 Making questions

Turn to the Interaction appendix.
Student A: look at section 20.
Student B: look at section 32.

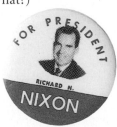

An interview

1 Interviewers

Sometimes a panel (or committee) interviews applicants for a job.
Imagine you're an applicant and look at this panel.

1 Which one is the chairperson?
2 Which ones look sympathetic?
3 Which ones look unsympathetic?
4 Which one has just asked a question?

How did you know the answers?

2 Interview questions

Read through these interview questions with a partner. What kind of
questions are they? For each sentence, decide which type of question it is
from the list below.

A Conversation opening (friendly) questions.
B Questions about skills and qualifications.
C Questions about your personality.
D Questions about salary and working conditions.
E Questions about your ambitions.

1 *Can you operate an IBM computer with Microsoft Windows?* .....
2 *Are you a loyal person?* .....
3 *What sort of job would you like in five years' time?* .....
4 *Do you want a job with a company car?* .....
5 *What do you do during your free time?* .....
6 *What things are you best at?* .....
7 *Did you have a good journey?* .....
8 *What grade did you get in your (word processing) exam?* .....
9 *How much are you hoping to earn?* .....
10 *What was the traffic like on the way here?* .....
11 *Would you like to have the same job in ten years' time?* .....
12 *Was it easy to find our offices?* .....
13 *Do you enjoy working with other people?* .....
14 *Would you like a cup of coffee?* .....

ER Shilton Hotel Group plc

We have a vacancy for a reception clerk at our new 4-star Portsmouth hotel and conference centre. Excellent salary and conditions.

Good standard of education required, with computer experience. One or more foreign languages an advantage. Overtime is necessary during holiday periods.

Apply in the first instance, enclosing CV to:
The Personnel Manager, The Shilton Harbour Hotel, Portsmouth, Hampshire, PO2 6FX

WORTHWELL

* Are you interested in a career in retail store management?
* We have vacancies for 16 trainee retail managers, to begin work in September!
* We offer full training in all areas of retailing.
* We offer an attractive salary and benefits with good prospects for future promotion.

Apply, enclosing CV to:
Mark G. Spencer, Training Officer,
WORTHWELL PLC
The Worthwell Building, Debenham Road,
Burton-on-Trent, NT23 6TW

IMMEDIATE VACANCY
FOR
Personal Assistant
for major rock star
on U.S. tour
See 43 states in 52 days!
And the money's great!
CAN YOU DO IT?
Apply with résumé to:
Virgil Kane Management Inc.
PO Box 15482
Atlanta, Georgia, USA

3 Job adverts

Read the adverts. What qualifications do you think the advertisers are looking for? What kind of work experience would be useful for these jobs?

4 Role-play

You are going to role-play an interview for one of the jobs. You can choose which one. The interviewer has your résumé. The interviewer is going to ask you other questions as well. You are also going to ask the interviewer some questions.

Turn to the Interaction appendix.
Student A: look at section 35. Student B: look at section 11.

Interview assessment

adverbs: manner and frequency

ASSESSING AN INTERVIEW:
QUESTIONNAIRE

1 *Look at the applicant's face during the interview. Which of the expressions below did the applicant have during the interview?*

- ☐ always the same
- ☐ shy
- ☐ nervous
- ☐ bored
- ☐ friendly
- ☐ interested
- ☐ unhappy
- ☐ worried

2 *How confident was the applicant?*

- ☐ over-confident
- ☐ confident
- ☐ quite confident
- ☐ not at all confident

3 *How often did the applicant smile during the interview?*

- ☐ all the time
- ☐ often
- ☐ hardly ever
- ☐ not at all

4 *How was the applicant sitting during the interview?*

- ☐ still
- ☐ moving a lot
- ☐ leaning forward
- ☐ leaning back

5 *Did the applicant do any of these things?*

- ☐ touching hair or clothes
- ☐ folding arms
- ☐ crossing legs
- ☐ waving hands
- ☐ showing the palms of their hands
- ☐ avoiding eye contact
- ☐ mirroring the interviewer's body language

6 *How did the applicant speak? You can tick more than one box.*

- ☐ spoke clearly
- ☐ didn't speak too loudly or too quietly
- ☐ didn't speak too quickly or too slowly
- ☐ answered questions well
- ☐ used good vocabulary
- ☐ sounded interested and enthusiastic

7 *How often did the applicant say 'er' or 'uh' or 'um' (or similar things)?*

- ☐ frequently
- ☐ quite often
- ☐ occasionally
- ☐ hardly ever

1 Observation

One pair comes to the front of the group or class and repeats the role-play interview from page 53. The rest of the class should complete this questionnaire.

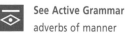

See Active Grammar
adverbs of manner

2 Presenting yourself again

Look back at the five facts about yourself which you wrote at the beginning of the unit. Do you want to change them?
Now present your facts again to the class as you did at the beginning of the unit.
Has your performance changed?

Understanding the structures

See Active Grammar

The past simple

The present perfect

Understanding the structures

1 The past simple – negatives and questions

Look at the examples and write answers in the same pattern.

Who did you speak to?
I didn't speak to anyone.

What did you say?
I didn't say anything.

1 What did you eat?
2 Who did they know?
3 What did you hear?
4 Who did she tell?
5 Where did they go?
6 What did he find?
7 Who did they meet?
8 Where did she sit?

Do you know the past tenses of all the verbs in the exercise?
Did you need to know the past tenses to do the exercise?
You can form negative sentences and questions with *did + bare infinitive*. You don't need to know irregular pasts to do this.

2 The past simple – affirmatives

You can answer questions without using the affirmative past simple.

Did you go there? Yes, I did.
When did you go? At 8 o'clock.

But for past statements and narrative you need to know the affirmative. Choose the correct form of the verb.

1 She (buy / bought) a CD yesterday.
2 They (see / saw / seen) the film last night.
3 We (come / came) to school early today.
4 He (wash / washed) his hair before he went to the party.
5 I (fly / flew / flown) to New York last year.
6 We (finish / finished) work an hour ago.
7 My test mark was 83% because I (know / known / knew) a lot of the answers.

3 Structure – the present perfect simple

Choose the correct words.

1 Have you ever (been / went / go) to Texas?
2 He (have / has) never been to Canada.
3 (Have / Has / Had) they finished yet?
4 She's lived in China (for / since) five years.
5 We've (yet / just) heard the news.
6 I've often (see / saw / seen) it on TV.
7 I've (already / yet) eaten it.
8 They (hasn't / haven't) done it yet.
9 Have you (do / done / did) everything yet?

4 Past tenses and past participles

Complete the spaces on this chart.

base	past	past participle
do	did	done
go	.....	gone
have	had	.....
think	.....	.....
.....	looked	.....
.....	.....	drunk
know	.....	.....
.....	fell	.....
write	.....	.....

5 Regular and irregular verbs

Are the sentences below true *(T)* or false *(F)*?

1 Most of the very frequent verbs in English (*come, go, be, have,* etc.) are irregular. .....
2 Newer verbs (e.g. *to video, to interface*) are always regular in the past. .....
3 In American English, a small number of past participles (e.g. *gotten, dove, snuck*) are different from British English. .....
4 Some verbs have both a regular and an irregular past form (e.g. *learnt / learned, burnt / burned*). .....
5 Technical and scientific verbs are regular.
6 English-speaking children use irregular forms when they begin to speak (*went, bought*), but when they get a little older they try to make the verbs regular (*goed, buyed*). .....

Past simple or present perfect?

1 Past simple and present perfect

Look at the sentences below. Some are finished or completed – write *PS* (past simple).
Others have some connection to the present. This connection can be a result of a past action, or knowledge we have now because of something we learned or saw in the past. It can be that the action hasn't finished yet, or that the time in the past was indefinite – write *PP* (present perfect).

1 The England team have beaten Scotland by three goals to two. .....
2 Gary Smith scored the first goal. .....
3 They have often met her. .....
4 She was here yesterday. .....
5 Sit down. I've just made a cup of tea. .....
6 Did you have a good journey? .....
7 Have you had lunch yet? .....
8 When did you have lunch? .....
9 Don't call Annie. I've already told her the news. .....
10 What did she say? .....
11 I had a big breakfast this morning. .....
12 Have you ever eaten fish 'n' chips? .....

2 Time words

The present perfect is not used for definite times in the past. Which of the words below are not normally used with the present perfect simple tense?

..... ago   ..... yet
..... already   ..... last night
..... since   ..... just
..... yesterday   ..... during
..... for three days   ..... at 6 o'clock

3 Adding information

We use the present perfect to make statements and ask questions in a general way, but we need to change to the past simple to give and ask for specific information:

A: *Have you ever met Mr Yakamoto?*
B: *Yes, I have. I met him last year.*

A: *Have you spoken to Paul recently?*
B: *Yes, I have.*
A: *When did you speak to him?*
B: *I spoke to him last night.*

Complete the spaces in these conversations.

A: Have you ever ..... to Florida?
B: Yes, I ..... .
A: When ..... you ..... there?
B: I ..... there two years ago.

C: Have you seen the new Disney movie?
D: Yes, I ..... .
C: What ..... you think of it?
D: It ..... pretty good. I ..... it. ..... you seen it?
C: Not yet. I'm going tonight.

4 Word order

Rewrite these sentences in the correct order.

been / Has / France? / ever / she / to
Has she ever been to France?

1 night? / you / Where / go / last / did
2 yet. / haven't / dinner / I / had
3 just / new / jacket. / bought / I've / a
4 morning. / got up / this / She / at / six
5 already / this / seen / I've / programme.
6 there / times. / I've / three / been
7 often / She / my / visited / has / house.
8 since / lived / They / here / have / 1995.

5 Learning vocabulary

When you learn new verbs, note down their three forms for irregular verbs (base, past, past participle), e.g. *see / saw / seen.*
If the verb is regular, you can note the sound of the ending ($/t/$ $/d/$ $/ɪd/$).

What would you say?

interacting
with strangers

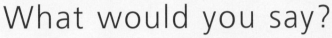

1

2

3

4

1 What are they saying?

What are the people in these pictures saying?
What would you say in the same situations?
Compare your ideas with the rest of the class.
How many ideas were there for each picture?

2 Categories

Put your sentences into these categories:
- apologizing
- making a suggestion
- offering help
- asking for permission
- refusing

5

indirect
questions

present perfect

have to

A cool reception

SECURITY OFFICER Excuse me! Sign here.
VISITOR Sorry?
SECURITY OFFICER You have to sign in. It's
the rules.
VISITOR But I haven't parked my car yet. I
can't get into the car park. The barrier's
down.
SECURITY OFFICER Have you got a parking
permit?
VISITOR No. I don't work here. I'm a
visitor.
SECURITY OFFICER Who are you visiting?
VISITOR Westchapel plc. They're on the
ninth floor.
SECURITY OFFICER Westchapel, eh? I've told
them before. They have to reserve
visitors' parking in advance.
VISITOR Maybe they have.
SECURITY OFFICER What's your name, then?
VISITOR Guthrie. Andrea Guthrie.
SECURITY OFFICER No. It's not in the book.
You can't park here.
VISITOR Well, where can I park? I've got a
meeting in five minutes.
SECURITY OFFICER I don't know. That's
your problem.
VISITOR I see. Thank you very much
indeed.

1 Before you listen

Make these words opposite by adding *un-*:

pleasant	sympathetic	co-operative
helpful	friendly	

2 Listening

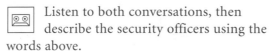 Listen to both conversations, then
describe the security officers using the
words above.

*The first one was unpleasant, but the other one
was pleasant.*

3 Analysing the conversations

Why did the second security officer give a
better impression? Find examples from the
second conversation of the following things.

1 He used a polite form of address.
2 He used a polite request.
3 He gave a reason when he asked her to
sign in.
4 He used an indirect question form.
5 He made an offer.
6 He was sympathetic.
7 He apologized.
8 He gave her advice.

Fifteen minutes later

SECURITY OFFICER Excuse me, ma'am. Would you mind signing in? It's a fire regulation, I'm afraid.

VISITOR Yes. of course. Sorry. I'm late for a meeting.

SECURITY OFFICER Can you tell me who you're visiting?

VISITOR Westchapel plc.

SECURITY OFFICER Hmm. They're on the ninth floor. I'll call them and tell them you've arrived.

VISITOR Thanks. I couldn't find a parking space.

SECURITY OFFICER I know. It's very difficult in this area. And we only have limited space in the car park.

VISITOR Mm. Uh … where's the other security officer?

SECURITY OFFICER Tom? It's his tea break.

VISITOR He wasn't very helpful.

SECURITY OFFICER I'm sorry about that. Look, next time you come here, why don't you park at the station? The car park's never full, and it's quite a short walk.

VISITOR I will. Thank you.

4 Vocabulary

Do you think the first security officer was doing his job well, or not? Talk about him. You can use the words below.

firm	rude	officious
aggressive	impatient	strict
impolite	efficient	careful

  See Active Grammar
indirect questions

5 Reading

JOBSWORTH

Several years ago there was an officious doorman at the BBC TV Centre in London who answered any request with the reply 'No, it's more than my job's worth!' He meant, 'If I let you do that, I'll lose my job.' The word 'jobsworth' became popular, and you can describe unhelpful doormen and security officers or other people in positions of authority as 'jobsworths'. Jobsworths never break, nor even bend, the rules!

Indirect questions

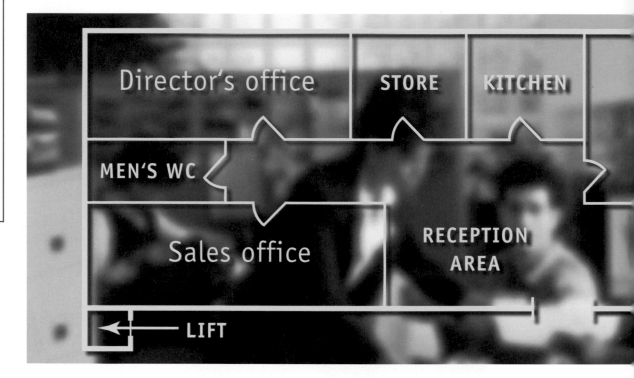

indirect
questions

giving
directions

cultural
awareness

1 Do you know where it is?

Listen to the conversation. Luke is a
sales representative. He is visiting the
offices of Westchapel plc. Tania is the
receptionist.

LUKE Good morning. I'd like to see Ms
Darwin.
TANIA Certainly. What's your name?
LUKE Luke Forster.
TANIA Ah, yes. She's expecting you, Mr
Forster. Do you know where her office is?
Luke No, I don't. I haven't been here before.
TANIA It's the third door on the right.
LUKE Thanks. Oh, could you tell me where
the men's room is?
TANIA It's at the end of the hall.

2 Asking for directions

Work with a partner. Ask about the picture of
the offices. Start at the reception area.

A: *Can you tell me where the Sales Office is?*
B: *Go left, and it's the first door on the left.*

3 Why use indirect forms?

Look at these two indirect questions.

1 *Do you know where her office is?*
   Can she change her question to *Where is
   her office ?*
2 *Could you tell me where the men's room is?*
   Can he change his question to *Where is the
   men's room ?*

So, why do we use indirect forms?
– because they sound more polite than direct
  questions
– because the other person may not know
  the answer

Which reason applies to example 1?
Which reason applies to example 2?

 See Active Grammar
indirect questions

4 Culture comparison

In some cultures (e.g. The Netherlands,
Poland, Scandinavia) people value directness,
while in other cultures (e.g. Japan, Britain)
people prefer to be more indirect. What do
people prefer in your country?

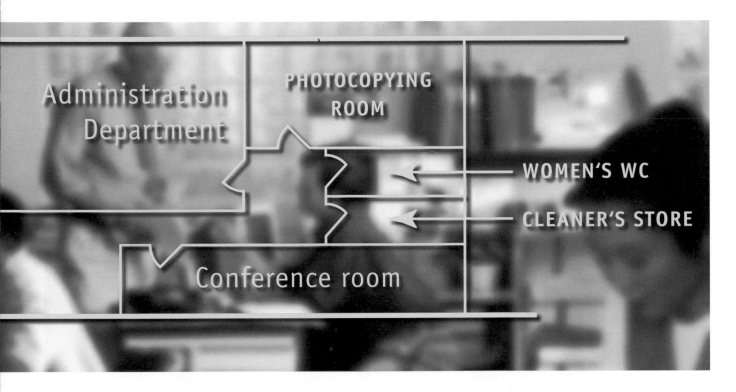

5 Asking about people

Work with a partner. Ask about the phone list, using indirect question forms.

WESTCHAPEL PLC

| THE MONTAGUE BUILDING | MANDELA STREET, SEATOWN | |

INTERNAL PHONE DIRECTORY:

Name	Department / Job	Extension
Darwin, Ms C	Managing Director	507
Hegel, Mrs E	Admin. Secretary	517
Locke, Ms T	Reception Clerk	501
Machiavelli, Mrs	Cleaner; teas	502
Mill, Ms JS	Office manager	514
Rousseau, Mr JJ	Computer Operator	508
Socrates Mr D	Sales Rep – South	515
Zappa Mr F	Accounts Clerk	513

A: *Do you know who Mrs Hegel is? / Can you tell me what Mrs Hegel does?*
B: *Yes, she's the administration secretary.*
A: *Could you tell me what her extension number is?*
B: *Yes, it's 517.*

6 Asking about appointments

This is an appointment book for next week.

MONDAY
10.00 *Ms Peters cancelled*
2.30 *Mrs Wilson*

TUESDAY
10.15 *Mr Forster*
10.30 *Miss Venables cancelled*
11.00 *Ms Hammond, Mr Lewis*

WEDNESDAY
12.45 *Mr Allen*

THURSDAY
9.00 *Mr Kelly*

FRIDAY
12.15 *Ms Stone cancelled*

Ask and answer with a partner.

Student A: It's your appointment book, but Student B is your assistant and makes all your appointments.

A: *Do you know if I'm seeing Ms Peters next week?*
B: *No, you aren't. / Yes, you are.*
A: *Can you tell me when I'm seeing her?*
B: *On Monday at ten o'clock.*

Offers

offers

accepting and
refusing offers

intonation

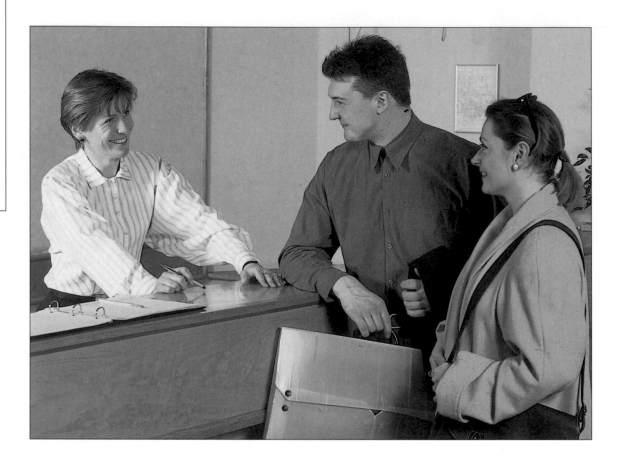

1 Welcoming visitors

 Tania is working in reception at Westchapel plc.

TANIA Good morning. Can I help you?

WOMAN Hello. Yes, Alice Hammond and Tim Lewis. Premier Design. We have an appointment with Ms Darwin at eleven. We're a bit early.

TANIA Ah, yes. She's still in a meeting. She won't be long. Shall I take your coats?

MAN Thank you.

TANIA Would you like to sit over here? I'll get you a drink while you're waiting.

WOMAN That would be lovely. Thank you.

TANIA Would you prefer tea or coffee?

WOMAN Tea, please.

MAN The same for me.

TANIA Do you take milk and sugar?

WOMAN No milk, no sugar, thank you.

TANIA And for you, Mr Lewis?

MAN Milk, two sugars, please.

Tania does these things. Find them in the dialogue.

1 She greets the visitors.
2 She offers to take their coats.
3 She invites them to sit down.
4 She offers them a drink.
5 She remembers the visitor's name.

The visitors do these things. Find them in the dialogue.

6 They introduce themselves.
7 They give a reason for being there.
8 They accept her offers.

2 Listening

Listen to these offers. Some offers sound sincere and genuine, and some offers sound insincere, or rude. Write ✓ (I'll accept the offer) when the offer sounds sincere, or ✗ (I'll refuse the offer) when the offer sounds insincere or rude.

1 I'll help you carry the cases. .....
2 Why don't you let us do the dishes tonight? .....
3 Would you like me to go to the shops for you? .....
4 I'll do it later. .....
5 Er, do you need any help? .....
6 Shall I make the coffee? .....
7 Look, come in and sit down. Leave it all to me. .....
8 Let me do it.
9 Can I help you across the road? .....

Can you reverse the meaning by using the tone of your voice? Try!

3 Accepting and refusing offers

Choose appropriate replies for the sentences in 2.

Accepting	Refusing
Thank you.	No, thank you.
All right.	No, that's all right, thank you.
That's very kind of you.	No, it's OK, thank you.
OK. Thank you very much.	I can manage, thank you.
That would be (lovely).	No, don't bother. I'll do it.

4 Conversation

Follow the instructions and have a conversation with a partner.

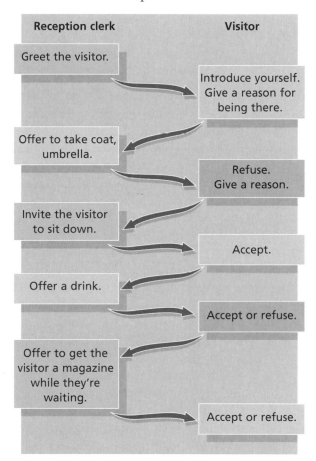

5 Role-play

Role-play a conversation with a partner.
A is B's teacher or B's boss. B left something behind in class or at work. A is returning it to B at B's home.

See Active Grammar
offers

suggestions
invitations
present perfect

Suggestions and invitations

1 Listening

Sarah Tollard is British. She's visiting Toronto on business. It's Friday afternoon, and she's in a meeting with Carol Davies.

Listen to the conversation, then fill in the gaps from memory.

CAROL … that's it, Sarah. We've finished. Are you flying back to England tonight?
SARAH ....
CAROL Have you been up the CN Tower yet?
SARAH No, not yet.
CAROL ....
SARAH That's very kind of you, Carol. But it's Saturday. I don't want to take up your time …
CAROL It's no trouble. I'd enjoy it.
SARAH ....
CAROL Of course! Now, would you like me show you the sights?
SARAH ....
CAROL It'll be fun. Is ten o'clock OK?
SARAH ....
CAROL Have you been to the waterfront?
SARAH No.
CAROL ....
SARAH Well, er… yes. OK.
CAROL ....

Practise the conversation with your partner. Then check with the Listening appendix.

2 Culture comparison

Notice that Sarah refuses Carol's invitation at first. Sarah is being polite. She wants to make sure that Carol is being sincere and that it won't be too much trouble for Carol. Refusing invitations, offers, and suggestions several times before accepting is a British habit. The Americans do this too, but usually accept a second invitation.

What do you do in your country?

3 Places to visit

Match these pictures of Toronto to four of the descriptions below.

A Ontario Place Marina
B The Parliament Building
C Union Station
D St James's Cathedral
E Ontario Science Centre
F The CN Tower
G The Eaton Centre Shopping Mall
H Queen's Park
I The Royal Ontario Museum
J The Skydome Sports Stadium

4 A visitor to your town

Imagine that a foreign visitor is in your town, and that you are going to show them around tomorrow. Think about what you are going to suggest. Make notes, using the prompts below.

– meeting time
– meeting place
– places to visit before lunch
– area to have lunch
– restaurant for lunch
– local speciality for lunch
– places to visit after lunch

5 Write the conversation

Work with a partner and write a conversation.
Demonstrate your conversation to the class.

Here are some expressions you can use:

Before you suggest ...	Suggesting and inviting ...	Accepting
Have you | been to ...?	I can (show you / take you to) ... , if you like.	That's a good idea.
seen ...?	Would you like to go to ...?	Yes, I'd love to ...
visited ...?	How | about (doing) ...?	All right. Let's (do that).
tried ...?	What |	
eaten ...?	Is (...) OK / alright?	**Refusing**
	Shall we (do) ...?	No, I'm afraid I can't.
Do you know ...?	Let's ...	Well, I'd rather not
Would you like to | see ...?	Why don't we ...	If you don't mind, I'd
try ...?	Why not ...	rather not.

 See Active Grammar

suggestions; invitations; present perfect

Apologizing

1 Body language

Look at the pictures.
Which of the people are apologizing?
What gestures do you use when you apologize?
Why are they apologizing in the pictures?
What are they saying in the pictures,
do you think?

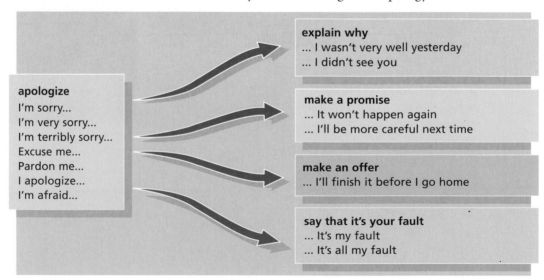

2 What are they saying?

Look at the chart. Notice that we usually add something to an apology.

apologize
I'm sorry...
I'm very sorry...
I'm terribly sorry...
Excuse me...
Pardon me...
I apologize...
I'm afraid...

explain why
... I wasn't very well yesterday
... I didn't see you

make a promise
... It won't happen again
... I'll be more careful next time

make an offer
... I'll finish it before I go home

say that it's your fault
... It's my fault
... It's all my fault

Match the two parts of these sentences:

1 I'm sorry I'm …   A   but I completely forgot.
2 I'm very sorry…   B   the mistakes. I'll correct them.
3 I'm terribly sorry, I …   C   late but I missed the bus.
4 I'm sorry about …   D   won't do it again.

3 Excuses

Here's a postcard that you can buy in Britain. Can you think of any more excuses?

INSTANT EXCUSE CARD!
Keep this card on your desk at all times!

When things go wrong, choose the best excuse:
1   I didn't do it.
2   Nobody asked me to do it.
3   It's not my job.
4   Nobody signed the authority.
5   I never received the order.
6   The computer broke down.
7   It was lost in the post.
8   No one said it was urgent.
9   I was away that day.
10 Don't worry. I'll do it now.

IMPORTANT!
Never take the blame for anything!

4 Listening

 Listen to these conversations.

Conversation 1: Does Naomi want to come to the party? Can she come? Does she give a reason? Do you think she is sincere?

Conversation 2: Do you think Tony is sincere? Is he telling the truth? Does he give a reason or an excuse?

Conversation 3: Annabel can't come. What reason does she give? Do you think she is sincere? Who does she offer to tell about the party?

Conversation 4: Complete these sentences from the conversation.
1 I have ..... appointment.
2 I can't come. I'm ..... .
3 Why didn't you ask me ..... ?
4 I'm sorry. It's my ..... .

Conversation 5: Complete the invitation card.

Please come to
JASON'S
Party on
Saturday 18th February
Time.........................
Place.........................

5 Use the Listening appendix

Now look at the Listening appendix. Highlight the invitations and apologies in the conversations. Then act out the conversations in pairs.

6 Improvisation

Improvise a telephone conversation in pairs. Student A invites Student B to a party. Student B can't come, and apologizes.

7 Group work

Work in groups. One student invites each of the others to a party. The others apologize and give different excuses.

8 Interaction

Work in pairs. Turn to the Interaction appendix.
Student A look at section 4.
Student B look at section 15.

Requesting permission

permission

conditional forms of modals

do you mind...

1 Polite formulas

Asking for permission is a type of request. Grade the formulas below.

*	not very polite
**	polite
***	very polite
****	extremely polite

..... Could I use your phone?

..... Might I possibly use your phone?

..... Sorry to trouble you, but do you mind if I use your phone?

..... Would you mind if I used your phone?

..... May I use your phone?

..... I'll use your phone, OK?

..... Can I use your phone?

..... I wonder if I could use your phone.

 See Active Grammar
permission

2 How do you choose the right formula?

Ask yourself these questions:

– Does the other person have higher status than you (e.g. more authority or older)?

– Is the other person a stranger, an acquaintance, a colleague, a friend or a relative? (You don't need polite formulas with people you know well - it sounds sarcastic.)

– Is your request going to cause the other person trouble or extra work?

– Is the other person in a good mood or a bad mood?

3 Giving permission

Is B giving permission or not?

1 A Is it all right if I open the window?
   B Go ahead.

2 A Do you mind if I turn on the light?
   B No, not at all.

3 A Do you mind if I smoke?
   B Yes, I do.

4 A Would you mind if I used your phone?
   B No, I don't mind.

5 A Am I allowed to park here?
   B Sorry, no.

6 A Can I borrow your calculator?
   B OK.

7 A Could I look at your newspaper?
   B Yes, you can.

8 A May I leave early tonight?
   B I'm afraid not.

9 A May I see your bank statement?
   B No, you may not!

10 A Might I ask you a personal question?
    B Yes, you may.

THE FAR SIDE By GARY LARSON

© 1986 FarWorks, Inc./Dist. by Universal Press Syndicate

"Mr. Osborne, may I be excused? My brain is full."

Rules and regulations

rules
prohibition
supposed to
passive
formulas

Hotel Splendide

For your safety:
Pool rules & regulations

1 **WARNING** – swim at your own risk – no lifeguard on duty
2 Pool reserved for hotel guests only
3 All children under 12 must be accompanied by adult
4 No running or games allowed in pool area
5 No food or drink permitted in pool area
6 No glass or bottles allowed in pool area
7 No animals permitted in pool or pool area
8 Guests must shower before entering pool
9 Maximum bathing load 66 persons
10 Maximum pool depth 2 metres
11 In case of emergency dial 0

*Telephones located in changing rooms
and next to bar*

DIVING STRICTLY PROHIBITED

Hey, you! You mustn't eat or drink in the pool!

Hey, guys, you're not allowed to bring food or drink into the pool area.

Dan! You're not supposed to eat in the pool area

1 Rules

Make complete sentences about the swimming pool.

No food or drink is permitted in the pool area.

  See Active Grammar
passives; articles

2 Telling people the rules

Which is the most officious? Which is the least officious?

You mustn't do that.
You can't do that.
Don't do that.
You're not allowed to do that.
You're not supposed to do that.

3 Interaction

  Work in pairs. Turn to the Interaction appendix.
Student A: look at Section 33.
Student B: look at Section 30.

4 Making the rules

Work with a partner. Think of lists of rules for:
– schools in your country
– driving in your country
– a sport or game

5 Breaking the rules

You're not supposed to copy CDs onto cassettes, but a lot of people do.

What rules do you / a lot of people regularly break in your country?

  See Active Grammar
allowed to / permitted to; supposed to

Saying the right thing

appropriate
language

politeness

PERSONALITY TEST

What would you do in these situations?

1 You're walking along on a train when you knock over someone's coffee. What would you say?

  A 'I'm terribly sorry.'
  B 'It's your fault! That was a stupid place to put it.'
  C 'Sorry. Are you OK? I'll get you another one.'

2 You arrive at the door of a department store at the same time as someone else. What would you do?

  A say 'After you'
  B say nothing, but walk through the door first
  C say 'Excuse me' politely, then walk through the door first

3 You're at work. You walk into an office. A colleague that you don't know very well is crying. What do you do?

  A say 'Sorry,' and leave the room
  B sit down next to them, say 'You look upset. Would you like to talk about it?'
  C say 'What's wrong? You're supposed to be working!'

4 You phone a colleague during the early evening about a work problem. They answer the phone and you can hear the sound of people talking. What do you say?

  A 'Sorry to call you at home. Are you having dinner? I can call later.'
  B 'I want to talk to you about a problem at work.'
  C 'Sorry to bother you, but it is important. We have a problem at work.'

5 Your company has a no smoking policy, which you agree with. A visitor walks into your office and lights a cigarette. What do you say?

  A 'You're not allowed to smoke here.'
  B 'Smoking causes cancer.'
  C 'I hope you don't mind, but I'm afraid we have a no smoking policy here.'

6 You're in a hotel and the TV in the neighbouring room is very loud. You're trying to get to sleep. What do you do?

  A knock on the wall with your shoe, and shout 'Turn that noise off! I'm trying to sleep!'
  B knock on the door of the neighbouring room and say, 'I'm sorry, but your TV's rather loud and I'm trying to sleep. Would you mind turning it down?'
  C call the reception desk and ask them to request your neighbours to turn their TV down

7 You're having coffee in a restaurant with an acquaintance. The bill arrives, and your acquaintance takes it. What do you say?

  A nothing
  B 'Thank you.'
  C 'Let me pay.'

8 Your colleague has won £10,000 in a lottery. What do you say?

  A 'Congratulations! That's wonderful!'
  B 'I never win anything!'
  C 'Can you lend me £100 until next month? I'll pay you back.'

Compare your answers with a partner then turn to section 12 on page 136 for scoring. After you've done this, you can find out what it means in section 18 on page 137.

The structure of modals

See Active
Grammar

ability

invitations

may, might

must / have to

obligation

offers

permission

requests

should

suggestions

will / shall

would like

1   Modal verbs and auxiliary verbs

Look at the sentences below. Underline the ordinary auxiliary verbs, and put a ring around the modal verbs (some people call these modal auxiliaries).

1   I don't like football.
2   'I can't swim very well.' 'Neither can I.'
3   Have you seen that new film?
4   We aren't going on holiday this year.
5   Was the phone ringing?
6   She must telephone her mother today.
7   'Did you know the rules?' 'Yes, I did.'
8   I may go out this evening.
9   Don't worry. I'll do the washing up.
10 You shouldn't drive so fast.
11 She doesn't work on Saturdays.
12 Could I borrow your pen, please?
13 Had you met him before?
14 It might rain later.
15 You haven't finished yet, have you?
16 They ought to repair this road.

2   What are the rules?

Look at these sentences. Six of them are rules about modal verbs. Two of them are not rules about modal verbs. Which two are not rules about modals?

– They don't take *-s* in the third person singular.
  She can do it. He might be there.
– They form questions, negatives, question tags, and short answers without using *be, have, do.*
  Must you go? I can't stay. Yes, you can.
– The past tense is formed by adding *-ed*, the present continuous is formed by adding *-ing.*
– After modals, we use the bare infinitive (the infinitive without *to*).
  I must tell them the news.
  It might be hot tomorrow.
  You should have a rest.

  Ought to is an exception.

– They do not have these forms: infinitives, present participles, past participles.
– They have contracted negative forms: *can't, mustn't, won't, shouldn't.*
– The contraction *shan't* is rare. The contraction *mayn't* is almost never used – we prefer *may not.*
– A short response to a question can be made by using *Yes, I have / Yes, I am / Yes, I do* or *Yes, I did.*
– *Will* and *would* have contracted affirmative forms: *'ll, 'd.*

3   Following the rules

Choose the correct words.

1   They might (be / to be) late.
2   He (cans / can) play the guitar.
3   (Must I / Do I must) take my passport?
4   I (may not / don't may) be at school tomorrow.
5   You'll call me, (don't you / won't you)?
6   We ought (leave / to leave) soon.

4   Which of them are modals?

Tick (✓) all the modals in this list:

..... have	..... can't	..... ought to
..... do	..... shall	..... prohibit
..... may	..... had	..... hasn't
..... didn't	..... won't	..... would
..... must	..... were	..... be able to
..... am	..... couldn't	..... supposed to
..... does	..... should	
..... will	..... want	..... have to
..... might	..... are	..... had better

5   Make the sentences negative

I can swim. *I can't swim.*

1   You should buy a new car.
2   It could be right.
3   I would like to be a teacher.
4   He might come to the party.
5   She may telephone tomorrow.
6   Anna will help you.

Using modals

1 Possibility and certainty

Match the sentence with a modal to the sentence with an adjective which has the same meaning. Write *A*, *B*, or *C* in the boxes.

1 It will happen. .....
2 It might happen. .....
3 It won't happen. .....
4 It must be true. .....
5 It can't be true. .....
6 It may be true. .....
7 It might be true. .....
8 It could be true. .....

A It's impossible.
B It's certain.
C It's possible.

2 *will, shall, would*

Match the sentences 1 to 6 with their function A to F.

1 Will you lend me £10?
2 I'll make you a cup of tea.
3 Would you like to come to a party with me?
4 Shall we sit over here?
5 You will do what you're told to do.
6 He will meet you at the airport.

an invitation A
an offer B
a command C
a request D
a suggestion E
an arrangement F

3 Ability

Look at the examples and write eight true sentences about yourself.

I can play the violin. / I can't drive.
I could swim when I was six. / I couldn't speak any English when I was eleven.

4 Advice

Should and *ought to* are about the same; *had better (not)* is very strong advice. Give advice in these situations.

– Someone wants to feel healthier and fitter.
– Someone wants to learn a foreign language.

5 Obligation

Do you have these rules in your country? Write short answers.

Must car passengers wear seat belts?
Yes, they must. / No, they needn't.

1 Must car drivers have insurance?
2 Must drivers switch on their lights when it's raining?
3 Must people carry identity cards?
4 Must young men do military service?

Note: *must* is used less in American English, where it means a very strong obligation; *have to* can always replace *must* in both British and American English – and it is not a modal.

Change the questions above from *must* to *have to* questions. Answer them with *Yes, you do. / No, you don't.*

6 Prohibition

Write down these things:

– something you mustn't do while you're driving
– something you mustn't use on a plane
– something you mustn't do at work

7 Permission

The choice of modal depends on how big the favour you are asking is: *could* and *may* are about the same; *can* is less polite; *might* is more polite.

Ask for permission / a favour in these situations. The choice of verb depends on your opinion of how big the favour is.

– You want to borrow 20p from a friend.
– You want to borrow £20 from an acquaintance or colleague.
– You want to drive someone's car.
– You want to leave work half an hour early.
– You want tomorrow afternoon off.
– You want the whole of next week off work.

Topics of conversation

present perfect
v past simple

frequency
adverbs

1 What do you talk about?

Here are the ten most frequent topics of conversation. Read the list, and add two more topics in the empty boxes. How often do you talk about these topics? Interview a partner and complete the chart with the words below. Ask your teacher to complete the chart as well.

nearly always / frequently / sometimes /
not often / hardly ever / never

TOPIC	How often?
the news / politics	
health, diet, or exercise	
sport	
relationships / feelings	
work / business	
the opposite sex	
music	
your family	
cars / mechanical things	
clothes	

2 Comparison

What do you talk about with:
– your family?
– male friends / female friends?
– work colleagues / school colleagues?

Collect the results from the class. Are there differences between what women and men like to talk about?

3 Project: Conversation log

Person	Topic
Neighbour	The weather
Server in coffee shop	Food
Maria (friend)	Plans for the day

Who have you spoken to today? What about?

I spoke to Yoshi on the way to class. We talked about sport. I've spoken to Ingrid during this lesson. We talked about yesterday's homework.

Choose a day during the next week. Make notes of the topics you talk about during the day (in your language or in English), and who you spoke to.

See Active Grammar
present perfect v past simple

comparison of
adjectives and
adverbs

should

present
continuous

imperatives

Women and men

1 Conversation styles

There has been research into women and men communicating. These are some of the differences the surveys found between women and men in conversation.

Write *men* or *women* in the spaces. Check with section 25 on page 139.

Do you think they are true? Discuss with your teacher.

2 Does it matter?

The research showed that men and women use different styles of communication. Are these differences important:
- at work?
- at home?
- when you're learning a language?

 See Active Grammar
comparison of adjectives; comparison of adverbs

_____ talk more about feelings and relationships. _____ talk more about things.

_____ use fewer adjectives than _____ , and describe things in less detail.

_____ ask fewer questions in conversation.

_____ rarely discuss their personal life.

_____ use more polite formulas than _____ .

_____ tell more jokes.

_____ interrupt more than _____ (three times more often).

_____ more often smile when listening. _____ more often frown.

_____ are more attentive listeners (smiling, nodding, agreeing).

_____ use a greater range of intonation than _____ .

_____ ask others for help less often than _____ .

_____ make more direct statements. They begin sentences with *It is ...*, *We will ...*

_____ get to the point of the conversation more quickly than _____ do.

_____ make more indirect statements. They begin sentences with *I think ...*, *I hope ...*, *I feel ...*

_____ use more quantifiers (words like *all, none, every, always*).

_____ use more qualifiers (words like *a bit, kind of*).

3 Advice

Choose a title for each list.

A How men can communicate better with women at work.

B How women can communicate better with men at work.

Change the imperatives to advice.

Don't interrupt.   *You shouldn't interrupt.*
Get to the point.   *You should get to the point.*

Do you think the advice is helpful, sexist or a load of rubbish?

 See Active Grammar
imperatives; *should, shouldn't*

Don't interrupt.
Don't give commands or orders. Make polite requests.
Use more eye contact.
Don't be afraid to ask for help.
Practise listening skills.
Never shout or use bad language.
Never make sexist jokes or comments.
Don't be afraid to talk about feelings.

Get to the point.
Don't talk about personal problems.
Don't allow people to interrupt you.
Don't apologize (unless you are wrong).
Be more assertive. Make more direct statements.
Don't feel hurt if co-workers disagree with you.
Don't speak too quietly.

4 Space invaders

Look at the picture and answer these questions:

Are the men talking to the women?
Are the women talking to the men?
Are the women talking to each other?
What about the men?
Which ones are leaning forward?
Which ones are leaning back?
Which ones have got their legs under the table?
Which ones are sitting closer together?
Which ones are sitting further apart?
Which ones are taking up more space?
Which ones are taking up less space?

5 Discuss

Do you think the men are talking more loudly than the women?
What do you think the men are talking about?
What do you think the women are talking about?
Do you think this is a typical situation?
Is it easier for you to talk to someone of the same sex?

active listening

intonation of
echo questions

Attentive listening

'In an audience only sixty per cent of the people are actually listening at any one time.'

1 Body language

When we're listening to someone, we need to show them that we're listening attentively. We use body language, and we use noises and agreeing formulas as conversation fillers to do this.

What body language do people use to show that they are listening to the speaker? Demonstrate the body language to your teacher.

2 Listening

Listen to these conversation fillers, and repeat them after the recording. Then listen to the conversation. Which of the fillers do you hear?

..... Oh	..... No
..... Uh-huh	..... Right
..... Mmm	..... I see
..... Ah	..... Oh, really
..... Yeah	

3 Echoing

Echoing is another way of keeping a conversation going. It's another type of conversation filler.

A: *I went to London.*
B: *London?*
A: *Yes, and …*

Listen to the way B uses echoing. Then listen again and you ask the echo questions instead of B.

4 Checking that you understand

Sometimes a speaker uses a rising intonation to check that listeners are following what the speaker is saying. This forces the listener to respond by making noises or eye contact or nodding. This technique is used more frequently in American English. Listen to the recording and give positive feedback – nod your head when you hear the checking intonation.

conversation
fillers

punctuation

Conversation fillers

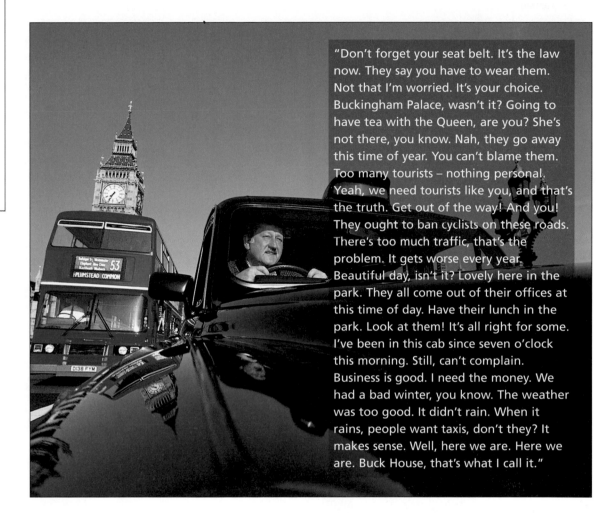

"Don't forget your seat belt. It's the law now. They say you have to wear them. Not that I'm worried. It's your choice. Buckingham Palace, wasn't it? Going to have tea with the Queen, are you? She's not there, you know. Nah, they go away this time of year. You can't blame them. Too many tourists – nothing personal. Yeah, we need tourists like you, and that's the truth. Get out of the way! And you! They ought to ban cyclists on these roads. There's too much traffic, that's the problem. It gets worse every year. Beautiful day, isn't it? Lovely here in the park. They all come out of their offices at this time of day. Have their lunch in the park. Look at them! It's all right for some. I've been in this cab since seven o'clock this morning. Still, can't complain. Business is good. I need the money. We had a bad winter, you know. The weather was too good. It didn't rain. When it rains, people want taxis, don't they? It makes sense. Well, here we are. Here we are. Buck House, that's what I call it."

1 Before you listen

You are a passenger in a London taxi cab, going to Buckingham Palace. Your driver likes talking. In this situation you need to use conversation fillers, whether you understand everything he says or not.

Decide where you might use conversation fillers. Put a slash (/) in the transcript of the driver's speech at these points. Choose appropriate conversation fillers. Compare with a partner.

2 Listening

Listen to the recording. Say your conversation fillers to yourself while you are listening. Does the driver pause in the places where you put a slash?

Listen to the recording again while one student demonstrates their conversation fillers.

3 Pair work

Student A describes a holiday. Student B uses any of the techniques on the opposite page while listening to Student A. They then change roles.

Pausing

punctuation
emphasis

Camilla and Diana are neighbours Camilla thinks that Diana is very quiet and that she never has anything to say Diana thinks that Camilla never stops talking neither of them is right they just have different personal styles Camilla speaks quickly and leaves short pauses for responses while Diana expects longer pauses in conversation interestingly Camilla is American and Diana is British generally British listeners expect longer pauses than American listeners

A woman from a small town in Arizona applied for a job in Washington DC at home everyone thought she was confident and friendly when she got to Washington people thought she was quiet and shy the problem was pausing in her home state people speak more slowly and they leave longer pauses for responses in Washington they speak faster and leave shorter pauses as a result she never had enough time for responses

Brandon comes from New York City but he has just moved to Alaska people think he is very aggressive and rude actually he's a very pleasant and polite person like people in most big cities New Yorkers speak quickly with short pauses when Brandon is listening to Alaskans he begins speaking as soon as they hesitate or pause they think he is interrupting them

1 Choosing pauses

When you are giving information, pauses are very important. If you speak without pausing, it's difficult for a listener to understand you.

Look at the three texts above. They have no commas, no full stops (periods), and no capital letters at the beginning of sentences.

Work in groups of three. Choose one of the texts each. Read the text silently. Think about pausing, then decide where to put commas, full stops and capitals.

2 Reading aloud

Take turns to read your text to the rest of the group. Remember:
– to pause
– to emphasize important words
– to make eye contact

The rest of the group should listen with the book closed.

can

it depends

Thinking time

1 Hesitation strategies

Often we want to give ourselves thinking time before we answer a question, especially if we don't understand it! Here are four techniques:

Techniques	Examples	Advantages	Disadvantages
Pretend you haven't heard	*Pardon?* *Sorry?* *Eh?*	Simple - only one word to remember.	Everyone does it.
Repeat the question	*You mean … what is forty-five divided by nine?*	Lots of thinking time.	Can you remember the question?
Use delaying noises	*Well…* *Um…* *Er…*	You can use them several times in the same sentence.	If you use them too often you sound stupid.
Use *it depends*	*It depends.* *It depends on (the situation).*	You will sound intelligent. (Stroke your chin at the same time).	You can only use it when there is more than one possible answer.

Don't forget that you can use more than one technique.

Sorry? You want to know what I think about this?
Well … um … it depends, really.

Ask your partner questions. Your partner tries to get thinking time. You can ask:
– mathematical questions *What's five hundred divided by twenty?*
– factual questions *What's the capital of Mongolia?*
– moral questions *Should we kill animals for their fur?*
– personal questions *Do you believe in Father Christmas?*

2 Does this happen to you?

Ask a partner these questions.

– *Do you interrupt people to correct their mistakes?*
– *Do you get angry when other people interrupt you?*
– *If there is a pause in a conversation, do you feel embarrassed?*
– *Do you say something to fill the pause?*
– *In a conversation, are you the first person to give an opinion?*
– *If you get bored by a conversation, do you change the topic, or do you remain quiet?*
– *Do you like to be the centre of attention (the person everyone is listening to)?*
– *Do you feel shy in a large group?*
– *Do you notice when some people in a group are too shy to speak?*
– *Do you try to include them in the conversation?*

Being diplomatic

indirect
statements

apologies

present perfect

The captain called the sergeant into his office. 'Come in, Sergeant,' he said. 'Private Smith is one of your men, isn't he?'

'Yes, sir,' said the sergeant.

'Well, I'm afraid I've just had some very bad news,' said the captain. 'It's Smith's wife. She's left him. She's gone to Australia. I want you to give him the news.'

'Yes, sir,' said the sergeant.

'Please be diplomatic,' said the captain. 'I want you to break the news gently. Smith's a very sensitive man. I don't want to upset him. Do you understand?'

'Yes, sir,' said the sergeant.

The sergeant went out. The soldiers were standing in a line.

'Attention!' shouted the sergeant.

The soldiers stood smartly to attention.

'Right! All those soldiers with wives in England – take one step forward! Not you, Smith! Stay where you are!'

The doctor walked over to the patient. She sat down beside the bed.

'Well, Mr Jackson,' she said, 'I've got the results of your tests.'

'Oh, thank you, doctor,' said the patient.

'There's good news and there's bad news,' she said, 'Which do you want first?'

'Oh, the good news,' said the patient. 'Definitely the good news.'

'OK,' said the doctor, 'I'll get straight to the point. Your test results show that you've only got three days to live.'

'Oh, no!' said the patient, 'If that's the good news, what's the bad news?'

The doctor looked down, 'I got the results two days ago.'

1 Break it gently

 Listen. Which is the best way of giving Private Smith the message?

1 SERGEANT Smith, Your wife has left you.

2 SERGEANT Smith, I'm afraid I have some bad news. I have to tell you that your wife has left you.

3 SERGEANT Come in and sit down, Smith. I'm afraid I've got some very bad news. It's your wife …

SMITH Oh, no! She isn't dead, is she?

SERGEANT No …

SMITH Oh, no! Has she had an accident?

SERGEANT No. She's left you.

2 Good news, bad news

 Listen. Did the doctor try to break the news gently?

Was there good news and bad news, or bad news and worse news?

Did the doctor 'get straight to the point?'

What was the point?

– You've got one day to live.

– You've got two days to live.

– You've got three days to live.

Mrs Green was 91 years old and she lived in an Old People's Home. Every week she bought a ticket for the National Lottery. One day she won first prize – twenty million pounds! The nurses didn't know how to tell her, so they called her doctor. 'Oh, dear,' he said. 'She's got a very weak heart. The shock could kill her. If you tell her the news directly, she'll have a heart attack and drop dead. I'll go and tell her myself. I'll be diplomatic.'

The doctor sat and talked to Mrs Green about the weather for five minutes. Then he said casually, 'Oh, by the way, there's a lot of news about the National Lottery prize. It's twenty million this week.'

Mrs Green laughed, 'Do you know something? I buy a ticket every week. Of course I'll never win, but it gives me something to think about.'

'Well,' said the doctor, 'What would you do if you won that much money?' And he laughed.

'I've thought about that a lot,' she said. 'I've got no relatives and I'm 91. I don't need that much money. You've been my doctor for thirty years and you've always been very kind. I would give half of it to you.'

At that news, the doctor had a heart attack, and dropped dead.

3 Getting to the point

Listen. Did the doctor get straight to the point? Why / why not?

What was the first thing the doctor talked to Mrs Green about?

What expression did he use to introduce the subject of the lottery prize?

How did he do this, directly or casually?

Was he diplomatic?

4 How to be diplomatic

These are ways of being diplomatic:

A Say something positive before you say something negative.
B Introduce negative points with an apology.
C Indirect sentences sound better than direct sentences.
D Don't get straight to the point (but be careful of misunderstandings).

Look at the examples , and label them *A*, *B*, *C*, or *D*.

1 BANK MANAGER Do you know that your account is overdrawn by £200, Mr Bennet? .....

2 SUPERVISOR I like your work on the new project, Anna. It's very interesting. But you haven't done the calculations correctly .....

3 FRIEND Isn't it a lovely day? Shall we go to the beach later? Oh, by the way, do you remember that CD I borrowed from you? Well, I've lost it .....

4 CO-WORKER I'm very sorry, but I forgot to give you a message yesterday .....

5 Reacting to news

Look at these reactions. Write *G* for reactions to good news, *B* for reactions to bad news.

..... Oh, no!   ..... That's cool / neat.
..... Great!   ..... I'm pleased to hear that.
..... Oh, dear.   ..... Congratulations!
..... How awful.   ..... I'm sorry to hear that.
..... Well done!   ..... That's terrible.

6 Role-plays

You have some news to give to your partner. One of you has a piece of good news, the other one has a piece of bad news. Turn to the Interaction appendix.

Student A: look at section 2.
Student B: look at section 29.

Turn-taking

avoiding
interruptions

too / very

1 Control strategies

Conversation is a turn-taking process and it is more difficult when there are several people in a conversation. Look at the photos, which show strategies for controlling a conversation.

2 Directing conversations

Look at these expressions for directing conversation in a formal situation, like a business meeting. Put them into three groups:
A including quiet people
B stopping interruptions
C keeping the conversation to the point

1 What's your opinion, Sam?
2 May I continue?
3 Let me finish.
4 Shall we continue?
5 Let's get back to the point.
6 You haven't said anything yet, Sam.
7 Do you want to add anything here?
8 I haven't finished my point.
9 Please allow me to finish.
10 Does anyone want to say anything before we move on?

But what did you think of her presentation, Anna?

1

The speaker can choose the next speaker. You can stop someone dominating the conversation and you can include quieter people.

She was quite right about the future of CD Rom ...

Absolutely.

But ...

2

You can stop someone interrupting by avoiding eye contact with them, and continuing eye contact with your partner in the conversation. Don't drop the volume of your speech (i.e. don't begin to speak more quietly).

> *Actually, I've just bought a high-speed CD Rom, and ...*

> *Let me finish ...*
> *The point I was trying to make about CD-Rom is ...*

3

If someone interrupts you, and you haven't finished making your point, tell them clearly. You can use phrases like:
Let me finish. / May I finish?
Excuse me, I haven't finished.
Just a moment / Hang on a second.

3 Social skills in conversation

Read through this checklist, and think about your personal conversation skills in your own language. If you're not too embarrassed, ask a partner if they agree with your opinion about yourself!

Non-verbal communication:
– Do you stand too close or too far away?
– Do you make too much eye contact or too little?
– Are you relaxed?

Your voice:
– Do you speak too loudly or too quietly?
– Do you speak clearly?

Conversation skills:
– Do you interrupt too often?
– Can you finish making your point without people interrupting you?
– Is your speech too formal or too casual for the situation?
– Do you take turns, or do you stay quiet for long periods, or do you dominate the conversation?
– Do you show that you're listening attentively?

 See Active Grammar
too / very

4

When someone won't stop talking, and you are not interested in what they are saying, you can avoid eye contact, turn away or look at something else. Do not use conversation fillers.

> *Anyway, the DP550- B model has a better access speed, and as I said to Robbie Spencer in Sales the other day...*

Interrupting

interruptions
present simple
past simple

1 Listen and read

SUPERVISOR Ah, there you are. Do you know what time it is? It's nearly ten o'clock. You're an hour late for work. It isn't the first time either. This is the third time this month! You do understand the company rules, don't you? We start at nine o'clock. Everyone else in the department gets here by nine. We all have to get buses or trains, and we don't miss them. We leave our homes in plenty of time. I'm afraid you'll have to speak to Mrs Macintosh about this. I'm sorry, but I have to report this to her. You know how she feels about punctuality. I haven't told her about the other times, but this is too much. You didn't even telephone to let us know!

The accusation

MUSEUM GUIDE Ah, yes. Come this way, everyone. This is the main picture gallery. There's a very famous drawing over there. It's by Leonardo da Vinci. As I expect you know, Leonardo da Vinci was Spanish and lived in Venice where he drew this picture in about 1603. Anyway, it was in the early seventeenth century. Leonardo was a genius and his most famous painting was The Mona Lisa which is in the Louvre Museum in Rome. The first owner of the painting was the King of England, and he put the painting on his bathroom wall. It's a bit expensive for a bathroom nowadays, isn't it?

Correcting the facts

2 Interrupting politely

You are going to practise interrupting. Here are some phrases:

> Actually …
> Excuse me …
> I'm sorry, but …
> I just want to say …
> May I interrupt here?
> Do you mind if I say something?

When you want to stop someone interrupting, don't pause for too long, don't lower your voice, and (if you want) you can refuse to be interrupted.

3 Interaction: The Accusation

Student A role-plays the supervisor, and reads text 1, **The Accusation.** Think about your pauses first. Remember that you can try to stop your partner interrupting you! Student B: look at the Interaction appendix, section 27, and try to interrupt Student A.

4 Interaction: Correcting the facts

Then Student B role-plays the museum guide and reads text 2, **Correcting the facts.** Look at the instructions in **3**.
Student A: look at the Interaction appendix, section 36, and try to interrupt B.

Questions

See Active Grammar

Indirect questions

question formation

question tags

question types

1 Question words

Look at the questions and answers. Complete the spaces with question words from the box.

When?	Why?	Which?	Whose?
Who?	What?	Where?	

1 '..... do you live?' 'Belfast.'
2 ' ..... are they?' 'They're mine.'
3 '..... is she doing?' 'Watching TV.'
4 '..... 's that?' 'My sister.'
5 '..... did you go there?' 'I wanted to visit the old castle.'
6 '..... one is yours?' 'That one.'
7 '..... did it happen?' 'Five days ago.'

2 *How …?* questions

Complete the spaces with words from the box. Use each word once only.

far	high	tall	long	hot

1 'How ..... have you travelled today?'
   'Nearly 400 kilometres.'
2 'How ..... is it?'
   'Over thirty degrees Celsius.'
3 'How ..... are you?'
   'About one metre eighty.'
4 'How ..... is it?'
   'Twenty-two centimetres.'
5 'How ..... is the mountain?'
   'Six thousand metres.'

3 Question tags

Add question tags to these sentences.

1 It's a beautiful day, ... ?
2 That restaurant looks good, ... ?
3 You haven't been there before, ... ?
4 You've tried English beer, ... ?
5 You didn't go out last night, ... ?
6 There wasn't much on TV, ... ?
7 You can understand everything, ... ?
8 It will be interesting, ... ?

4 Paying attention

We often ask short questions to show that we are listening carefully to a speaker.

A: *I liked the film.*
B: *Did you?*

We don't usually expect an answer. We can also use expressions like *Really?*, *Oh, yes?*, or *Is that so?* for the same purpose. Write short attention questions.

1 We didn't watch TV last night.
2 We went to a concert.
3 My sister likes Beethoven.
4 I can't stand his music.
5 The concert wasn't very good.
6 The orchestra were playing very loudly.
7 I've got a headache today.

5 Echo questions

We can show we're paying attention by using echo questions. We can repeat the whole statement with a question intonation, or simply repeat the last word or words.

A: *I went to London.*
B: *You went to London? / To London? / London?*

Ask short echo questions for these statements.

1 I've just come back from America.
2 I stayed in Washington D.C.
3 I was there for ten days.
4 We went to the Air and Space Museum.
5 They've got the original Apollo 11.

6 Question intonation with statements

Sometimes we want to check that listeners are paying attention. In informal conversation people often use a small rising question intonation when they make a statement. Read this passage with a small rising question intonation for each statement.

> He's in a new movie by Stephen Speilberg. He's just moved to Los Angeles. And he's bought a house on Mulholland Drive. It's near Universal Studios.

Indirect forms

1 Word order with direct questions

Rewrite these direct questions in the correct order.

1 begin? / the / What / programme / does / time
2 Scotland? / ever / to / Have / been / you
3 did / say? / What / you
4 she / speak / Can / well? / French
5 mean? / word / this / does / What
6 train / time? / Did / on / leave / the

2 Indirect *Wh-* questions

Indirect questions do not follow the normal question word order.

Direct	Indirect
What is it?	Do you know what it is?

Choose the correct words.

1 Do you know where (was it / it was)?
2 Can you tell me what (they are / are they) doing?
3 Do you know what (Maria has / has Maria) done?
4 Have you got any idea when (it will / will it) begin?
5 Do you know which one (should I / I should) choose?
6 Can you tell us where (were Ann and Jeff / Ann and Jeff were) going?

3 Indirect *Yes / No* questions

Direct	Indirect
Is it raining?	Do you know if it's raining?

Transform these direct questions into indirect questions.

1 Is that her bag?
2 Can Paul speak English?
3 Was her flight on time?
4 Would they like something to eat?
5 Has she seen John today?
6 Will Mr Steel be here next week?

4 Wh- questions with *do / does / did*

Direct	Indirect
Where does she live?	Do you know where she lives?
What did he say?	Do you know what he said?

Transform these direct questions into indirect questions.

1 When does the train leave?
2 Where do they sell tickets?
3 Where did Anna go yesterday?
4 What did she do?
5 What did they see?

5 *Yes / No* questions with *do / does / did*

Direct	Indirect
Did he see it?	Do you know if he saw it?

Transform these direct questions into indirect questions.

1 Did that man buy anything?
2 Does she like rock music?
3 Does the bus stop here?
4 Did they go to London?
5 Did it rain yesterday?

6 Indirect statements

Indirect statements follow the same rules as indirect questions. Choose the correct words.

1 I've got no idea whose (is it / it is).
2 I know where (can you / you can) buy one.
3 I don't know whether (it's / is it) mine.
4 Susan didn't tell me where (she was / was she) going.
5 I can't explain why she (went / did go).
6 I don't know if (are they / they are) home.

7 Introducing indirect forms

Look back at the exercises and do them again quickly. Replace *Do you know …?* with *Can you tell me …?* and *Have you got any idea …?*

Then do **3** and **5** again. Replace *if* with *whether*.

describing
actions

present
continuous

Ways of presenting information

1

2

3

4

5

You can present information formally (e.g. a lecture, a sales presentation) or informally (e.g. telling a story, explaining or describing something).

Work with a partner. What are the people doing in the pictures? Choose from the list below.

Picture 1: A: *I think he's giving a lecture.*
            B: *And I think he has just told a joke, because the audience is laughing.*

- giving a lecture
- giving information
- giving instructions
- explaining something
- selling something
- telling a joke

- talking about themselves
- describing someone or something
- describing a process
- talking about something that happened
- telling a story

instructions

Explaining something

1 A puzzle

Have you ever done a jigsaw puzzle?
Do you enjoy doing jigsaw puzzles?
Can you find these pieces?
– a corner piece
– an edge piece
– a piece which is upside-down
– some pieces which are the right
  side up

2 A logical sequence

Think about how you do a jigsaw puzzle.
Number these stages from 1 to 9. Compare with a partner.

..... Put in the last piece to complete the puzzle.
..... Look at the box and find out how many pieces there are, and how
  big the puzzle is.
..... Open the box and take out the pieces.
..... Find the four corner pieces and all the edge pieces.
..... Put some of the pieces into colour groups.
..... Join the edge pieces together. Join the pieces which are easy to
  identify.
..... Continue, but leave the difficult pieces until the end.
..... Find a clear area which is large enough for the completed puzzle.
..... Turn all the pieces the right side up.

conditionals
type 1

*when, while,
before*

Giving instructions

1 Breathing

If you take shallow breaths, you will feel nervous and your voice will sound higher. If you breathe deeply you will feel relaxed and your voice will sound deeper and have more authority. There are many simple breathing exercises that you can do before speaking to a group of people. Here are two sets of instructions for the same exercise.

Work with a partner. You should both try the exercise. Student A follows the instructions on the left. Student B follows the instructions on the right.

In this exercise you should remember to breathe in through your nose while slowly raising your arms to the level of your shoulders. It is important to hold your breath for a short time before breathing out slowly through your mouth. You should be lowering your arms at the same time. When you have breathed out fully, remember to wait for a short time before repeating the exercise. You will need to continue for some time. You should make sure that you are breathing deeply. If you are, your stomach rather than your chest will expand. You can check this by placing your hands over your stomach and trying a few breaths before beginning the exercise.

The Art of Public Speaking
Dame Evelyn Irving

BREATHING EXERCISES

Do you breathe deeply? Before you begin the exercises, check that you can breathe deeply. Place your hands on your stomach and breathe. Your stomach (not your chest) will expand if you are breathing deeply.

EXERCISE 1
1 Place your hands by your sides. Breathe in slowly through the nose for 3 or 4 seconds.
2 While you're breathing in, raise your arms to shoulder level – parallel to the ground.
3 Hold your breath in for 3 or 4 seconds.
4 Breathe out slowly through the mouth for 3 or 4 seconds while lowering your arms.
5 Pause, without breathing in, for 3 or 4 seconds.
6 Start again and continue doing this for at least 2 minutes.

Relax! Breathing for Life
Dave Marsden

2 Giving instructions

Which set of instructions was easier to follow?

Here are some points about giving instructions:
– Break the instructions into a number of steps or stages.
– Present the steps in a logical order.
– Use clear direct language.

3 Ways of relaxing

How do you relax? Can you give instructions or advice about your favourite method?

See Active Grammar
conditionals – type 1

sequence
words

Describing a sequence

1   Arriving by air

Look at the photographs, and number the paragraphs opposite in the correct order from 1 to 6.

2   Recall

Write the numbers 1 to 6 on a piece of paper. Close the book and try to remember the six things which were in bold, and write them next to the correct numbers on your list. Check with a partner.

3   Sequence words

Use the list you have just made. Explain what happens at an airport to a partner. Student A explains the first three stages, Student B explains the last three. Use the sequence words below:

First ...
First of all...
Next ...
Then ...
After you have (done this),
(do that) ...
Finally ...

..... At Passport Control there are often two routes, one for citizens of the country, the other for non-citizens (or aliens). **THE IMMIGRATION OFFICER** will check your passport (and take your landing card if you have one), and may ask you questions. In some countries they will put a stamp in your passport.

..... As soon as you leave the plane, follow the signs to **PASSPORT CONTROL** (or Immigration). At international airports these signs will be in English as well as the local language.

..... Collect your luggage and look for the sign to **CUSTOMS**. In most countries the signs are red for *Goods to Declare* and green for *Nothing to Declare*. In the European Union there is also a blue sign for travellers from other European Union countries.

..... After you have been through passport control, **FOLLOW THE SIGNS** to the Baggage Hall. There will usually be a picture of a suitcase on the sign.

..... After Customs look for the **EXIT**. If someone is meeting you they will be waiting at the Meeting Point. You will see signs for taxis, buses or trains that will take you to your destination.

..... In the **BAGGAGE HALL** there may be several carousels. There will be TV monitors which show you the right carousel for your luggage, e.g. *AC 862 Toronto – 4*.

Looking at facts and figures

past continuous v
past simple

while

figures

1 Figures

 Can you say these things aloud in English? Check with the recording.

53%	3.721	6 - 2 = 4
16,000,000	3,700	25 ÷ 5 = 5
253,491	5.9	33 x 3 = 99
40,000 sq.km.	2,000,000,000	2 ½
0.5%	4 + 3 = 7	33 ⅓

2 Electricity consumption

Look at the graph. Ask questions.

Was electricity consumption increasing or decreasing at 6pm?
It was decreasing.

3 Audience share

Look at the pie chart. Make sentences.

Thirty-six per cent watched ITV.

4 Sunset times

Look at the table. Ask questions.

What time did the sun set on the twenty second of April?
It set at seven minutes past eight.

5 TV programmes

Look at the timetable. Ask questions.

What time did 'True Lies' begin?
It began at nine thirty/ half past nine.
When did it finish?
It finished at eleven thirty / half past eleven.
How long was it?
Two hours.
What was on Channel 4 at eight o'clock?
Brookside.

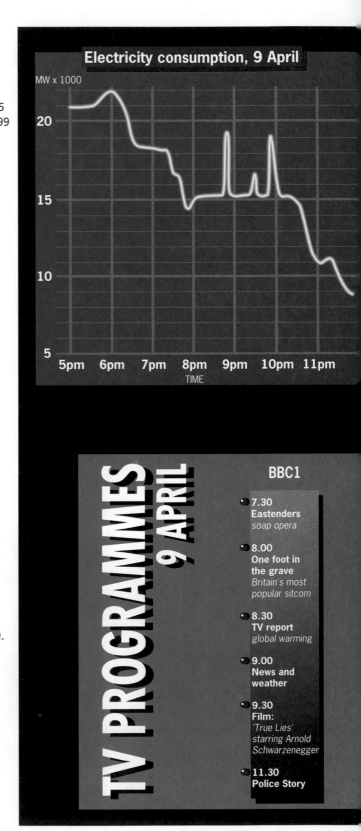

Electricity consumption, 9 April

MW x 1000

20

15

10

5

5pm 6pm 7pm 8pm 9pm 10pm 11pm

TIME

TV PROGRAMMES
9 APRIL

BBC1

7.30
Eastenders
soap opera

8.00
One foot in the grave
Britain's most popular sitcom

8.30
TV report
global warming

9.00
News and weather

9.30
Film:
'True Lies'
starring Arnold Schwarzenegger

11.30
Police Story

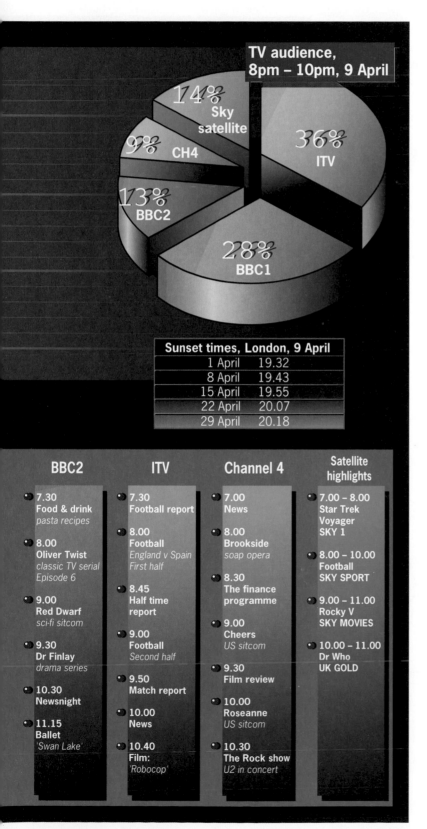

TV audience, 8pm – 10pm, 9 April

- 14% Sky satellite
- 9% CH4
- 36% ITV
- 13% BBC2
- 28% BBC1

Sunset times, London, 9 April

1 April	19.32
8 April	19.43
15 April	19.55
22 April	20.07
29 April	20.18

BBC2	ITV	Channel 4	Satellite highlights
7.30 Food & drink *pasta recipes*	**7.30** Football report	**7.00** News	**7.00 – 8.00** Star Trek Voyager SKY 1
8.00 Oliver Twist *classic TV serial Episode 6*	**8.00** Football *England v Spain First half*	**8.00** Brookside *soap opera*	**8.00 – 10.00** Football SKY SPORT
9.00 Red Dwarf *sci-fi sitcom*	**8.45** Half time report	**8.30** The finance programme	**9.00 – 11.00** Rocky V SKY MOVIES
9.30 Dr Finlay *drama series*	**9.00** Football *Second half*	**9.00** Cheers *US sitcom*	**10.00 – 11.00** Dr Who UK GOLD
10.30 Newsnight	**9.50** Match report	**9.30** Film review	
11.15 Ballet *'Swan Lake'*	**10.00** News	**10.00** Roseanne *US sitcom*	
	10.40 Film: *'Robocop'*	**10.30** The Rock show *U2 in concert*	

6 Find this information

1 The title of Britain's most popular sitcom.
2 The name of the star of 'True Lies'.
3 The title of a BBC1 soap opera.
4 The channel showing a classic TV serial.
5 The number of channels which were showing football.
6 The starting time of BBC's drama series.

7 While you're watching TV

Which of these things do you do while you're watching TV?

I (sometimes) eat snacks while I'm watching TV.

- read
- have dinner
- do homework
- write letters
- eat snacks
- speak on the telephone
- change channels frequently
- go to sleep

8 Explanations

Look at the graph. There was a peak on the graph at 8.45. Can you explain this?

The football match started at 8. Between 8 and 9 a lot of people were watching the football match. At 8.45 the game stopped. It was half-time. In millions of homes, people switched on lights, made hot drinks and went to the bathroom. Electricity consumption increased sharply because it was half-time.

Explain why these things happened:

1 There was a sharp decrease after 6 o'clock.
2 Consumption was decreasing between 7.30 and 7.50.
3 Consumption increased slightly just before 8 o'clock.
4 Consumption rose sharply at 8.50.
5 Consumption also increased sharply at 9.50.
6 Consumption fell between 10 and 11.
7 Consumption was low after 11.30.

See Active Grammar
past continuous v past simple

past perfect
during
signalling
let's

Presenting facts and figures

1 Find the answers

1 Name **three** developed countries.
2 Name three developing countries.
3 Find **a** word which means 'destruction of forests'.
4 Where did nuclear accidents happen between 1972 and 1992?
5 How much had the world population increased during this period?
6 How many cities had grown to over 10 million people during this time?
7 What percentage of the rainforest was destroyed during 1972?
8 What percentage of the rainforest was destroyed during 1992?
9 Look back at the questions. How many ways can you find of saying '1972 – 1992'?

 See Active Grammar
past perfect; *during*

2 Signalling

When you are presenting information, you need to give the audience signals.

Functions	Signals
Introductions	I'm going to talk about … My topic / subject is …
Sequencing	First … Next … / Then … / After that … (The /My) next point is … Finally …
Changing topic	Now let's look at … Now let's turn to …
Giving examples	For example … As you can see from (the picture)… The (graph /chart) shows …
Conclusions	In conclusion … To sum up …

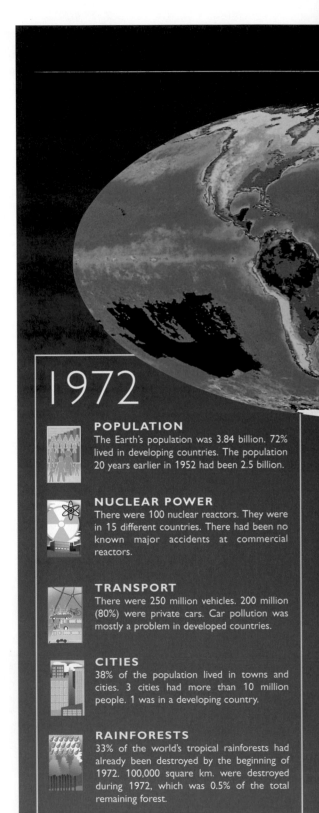

1972

POPULATION
The Earth's population was 3.84 billion. 72% lived in developing countries. The population 20 years earlier in 1952 had been 2.5 billion.

NUCLEAR POWER
There were 100 nuclear reactors. They were in 15 different countries. There had been no known major accidents at commercial reactors.

TRANSPORT
There were 250 million vehicles. 200 million (80%) were private cars. Car pollution was mostly a problem in developed countries.

CITIES
38% of the population lived in towns and cities. 3 cities had more than 10 million people. 1 was in a developing country.

RAINFORESTS
33% of the world's tropical rainforests had already been destroyed by the beginning of 1972. 100,000 square km. were destroyed during 1972, which was 0.5% of the total remaining forest.

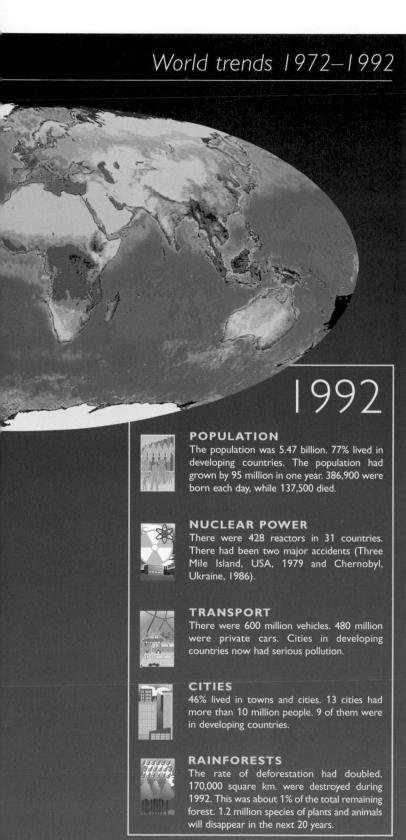

World trends 1972–1992

1992

POPULATION
The population was 5.47 billion. 77% lived in developing countries. The population had grown by 95 million in one year. 386,900 were born each day, while 137,500 died.

NUCLEAR POWER
There were 428 reactors in 31 countries. There had been two major accidents (Three Mile Island, USA, 1979 and Chernobyl, Ukraine, 1986).

TRANSPORT
There were 600 million vehicles. 480 million were private cars. Cities in developing countries now had serious pollution.

CITIES
46% lived in towns and cities. 13 cities had more than 10 million people. 9 of them were in developing countries.

RAINFORESTS
The rate of deforestation had doubled. 170,000 square km. were destroyed during 1992. This was about 1% of the total remaining forest. 1.2 million species of plants and animals will disappear in the next 20 years.

3 A presentation

Look at the short presentation below. Find the signals in the talk and underline them. What is the function of the signals?

I'm going to talk about the increase in the size of cities – cities are getting much bigger. I'm also going to talk about the increase in the number of large cities – there are more big cities now than twenty years ago. First, let's look at the figures. In 1972 only three cities had more than ten million people. Let's look at 1992. In that year there were thirteen cities with more than ten million, for example Mexico City, Tokyo, and Shanghai. Next, I'm going to look at the number of people who lived in cities. In 1972, thirty-eight per cent lived in towns and cities. Let's turn to 1992. The number had increased to 46% . Finally, let's look at developing countries. In 1992 nine of the thirteen biggest cities were in developing countries. To sum up, by 1992 the number of major cities had increased and more people were living in urban areas.

4 Group work

Look at 'World trends 1972 – 1992'. Each of you is going to give a talk. Make notes before you begin. You can add extra facts if you know them.

Student A talks about population.
Student B talks about nuclear power.
Student C talks about transport.
Student D talks about rainforests.

Before you give the talk to your class, do the breathing exercise on page 89.

5 Discussion

How do these trends affect your community? Do you ever discuss these trends?

Narrating

1   Reading

Tuesday, June 11

FAKE TRAFFIC COP ON THE M25

MICHAEL MELLOR got a four month suspended jail sentence for his hobby yesterday. Mellor is a sales representative who drives 400 miles a week on the M25 London orbital motorway. His hobby? Mellor dresses as a police officer, and stops motorists who are driving badly. He gives them a lecture on driving well, then warns them to drive carefully in future.

Mellor got the idea while he was driving home after he had been to a funeral. He was driving his white Ford Sierra along the M25, and he was wearing a white shirt and a black tie. He suddenly noticed that cars were going more slowly when they saw him. Police patrols on the M25 use plain white Sierras, and the police officers always wear white shirts and black ties. Two weeks later, a car overtook him on the wrong side. It was going very fast. Mellor was angry, and flashed his lights. The other car stopped. Mellor stopped too, and the other driver began apologising for what he had done. He called Mellor 'officer'.

Mellor bought a police cap and a fluorescent yellow jacket, like the ones used by the police. For eight months, Mellor patrolled the M25, and stopped dangerous drivers. At last, the real police saw him, and he was arrested. Mellor had to pay a £200 fine and lost his job. He said, 'I am very sorry ... I have no intention of doing it again.'

2 Comprehension

Answer the following questions about the text.

1 What was Mellor doing when he got the idea?
2 Where had he been?
3 What make of car was he driving?
4 What was he wearing?
5 What did he notice?
6 What happened two weeks later?
7 How long did Mellor patrol the M25?
8 What happened to Mellor in the end?

3 Adjectives and adverbs

Underline the adjectives in the story.
Put a ring around the adverbs in the story.

a car overtook him on the <u>wrong</u> side. It was going very (fast).

4 Describing

Work with a partner. You can make descriptions more interesting by adding adjectives and adverbs.

A car overtook him on the wrong side.

Student A:
A red car overtook him on the wrong side.
Student B:
A large red car overtook him on the wrong side.
Student A:
A large red car overtook him dangerously on the wrong side.
Student B:
A large red sports car overtook him dangerously on the wrong side.
Student A:
A large red sports car overtook him fast and dangerously on the wrong side …

Do the same with these sentences:
– Mellor is a sales representative.
– He stops motorists who are driving badly.
– He was wearing a white shirt and black tie.
– Mellor was angry, and flashed his lights.
– Mellor bought a police cap and a fluorescent yellow jacket.

5 Discuss

Why do you think Mellor did this?
Was it because he wanted power or because bad driving made him angry?
Do you think he did any harm? Why? / Why not?
Elvis Presley had the same hobby. He went on patrol with police officers, and stopped dangerous drivers. Would you like to do this?

6 Which past tense?

Choose the correct words to complete this story.

When I got to the bus stop, the bus (had gone / went), so I was late. When I arrived at Suzy's house, she (was / had been) surprised to see me. I gave Suzy the present I (bought / had bought) the day before. Suzy (liked / had liked) the present. There (was / had been) nobody else at Suzy's house. It was the wrong day! Her birthday party (was / had been) the week before. I (hadn't looked / didn't look) at the invitation carefully.

7 When do you use narration?

Which of the following things include *narration*?

– talking about your career
– talking about the history of your company
– talking about trips to other cities and countries
– talking about people you have met
– reporting things you have read in the paper / seen on TV / heard on the radio
– telling stories about yourself
– telling stories about other people
– telling jokes

 See Active Grammar
past perfect v past simple

narrative
tenses

adjectives

Making a story interesting

1 Urban legends

Urban legends are stories that you hear from friends. They are told as true stories, but the same 'true' story appears in many different versions. Look at this basic version of an urban legend. Boring isn't it? When people tell urban legends they try to make their story interesting by adding details.

> Someone had bought a well-known food or drink product. While they were eating or drinking it, they found something in the product. They wrote to the manufacturer who asked them to keep quiet about it and gave them something.

 See Active Grammar

adjectives

2 Adding detail

What kind of detail can you add? Look at the table below. Listen to a different version of the story, and put a ring around the details that the narrator mentions.

Who did it happen to?
A friend of mine
Someone I know
A friend of my sister's
My cousin
My friend's hairdresser

When did it happen?
Once
One night
A few years ago
A few months ago
Last summer
Two months ago

Where did it happen?
Near my town
In a park
The Red Lion restaurant in the High Street
At a cinema
On the road from London to Dover

What were the consequences?
She was really ill
She couldn't work
She was hurt
He was nearly killed
She lost a lot of money
She nearly died

What's the punch line?
They gave her £5
They sent her another bottle
So she told the newspapers
She got £5,000

3 Interaction

There are some basic urban legends in the Interaction appendix, Work in groups, choose a story and tell it. Add details.
Student A: look at Section 7.
Student B: look at Section 16.
Student C: look at Section 37.
Student D: look at Section 1.

Then discuss the stories. Have you heard versions of these stories before? How was the version different?
Do you know any more stories like this?

narrative
tenses

reflexive and
emphatic
pronouns

dictionary skills

Humour

1 Ways of expressing humour

We can express humour in several ways:
- the way you say something
- facial expression and body language
- telling a joke
- telling an anecdote
- telling a story about yourself

2 Listening

Listen to these three recordings. Which is an anecdote (A), a joke (J), saying something humorously (H)? Write A, J, or H below.

1 .....   2 .....   3 .....

---

joke /ˈdʒəʊk/ noun **1** [C] something said or done to make you laugh, especially a funny story
Have you heard the joke about the three men in a taxi?
humour (US humor) /ˈhjuːmə(r)/ noun [U] **1** the funny or amusing quality or qualities of somebody / something
It's an awful situation, but at least you can see the humour of it. **2** being able to see when something is funny and to laugh at things
Rosie has a good sense of humour.
anecdote /ˈænɪkdəʊt/ noun [C] a short interesting story about a real person or event

---

3 Reading

 Beware of telling jokes at the wrong time and on the wrong subject. Sexist or racist jokes have no place in any conversation. People telling jokes of this kind are saying a lot about themselves, and what they're saying will give others a bad opinion of them.

 Jokes kill conversation. Someone tells a joke. People laugh. The conversation has stopped. There is silence. Then someone else has to tell another joke. The process repeats itself.

How to be successful in life
Dr Lauren K. Beckenbauer

See Active Grammar

reflexive and emphatic pronouns

4 Discuss

Do you agree with Dr Beckenbauer? Perhaps she didn't make a difference between a joke and an anecdote or humorous story.

narrative
tenses

Telling a funny story

1 A new car

  Listen and read.

A man had bought a new car, and he was very proud of it. There was only one problem. There was an irritating noise – a rattle – in the front of the car. The man had taken the car to a garage several times, but they couldn't find anything wrong with it. After several months they found the problem and explained it to him. The man was a non-smoker. He used the ashtray to keep small change for car parks and parking meters. He kept several pounds in the ashtray in 20p and 10p coins. That was the cause of the rattle. They hadn't discovered this before, because every time the man had taken his car to the garage, he had removed the money from the ashtray. He didn't trust the mechanics – he thought they might steal it. The last time he took the car to the garage he forgot to remove the money.

2 Change the details

Retell the joke to a partner. You can add details.

What make was the car?
Which garage was it?
When did this happen?

Work with a partner.

Student A:
Tell the same joke about a woman owner. Is the joke now sexist?

Student B:
Tell the same joke in the first person, i.e. it's a story about yourself. Is the joke funnier now?

3 Retelling a story

Do you remember the story about the twins in the listening on page 99? Retell it, but change some of the facts.
- Perhaps it was a famous visitor, not a school inspector.
- Perhaps there were three children, not two. Then the punch line becomes *quads*.

Do you remember 'Fake Traffic Cop on the M25,' the story earlier in this unit? Don't look back at it! Work in pairs and try to tell the story from memory. Begin:

I saw a story in the paper this morning …

Then turn back, and read the story again. What differences were there?

4 Who tells jokes?

Which of these people are likely to tell a joke in your country?
- a politician during a TV interview
- a sales representative
- a teacher during a lesson
- a senior business person during a meeting
- a doctor during a medical examination
- a man to a woman
- a woman to a man

5 Tell a joke

Tell a joke in English. (You can translate a joke from your language.)

Past tenses

See Active Grammar

during

past continuous

past participles

past perfect

past perfect continuous

past simple

1   Which tense?

Look at these sentences. Are they past simple (write *PS*), past continuous *(PC)*, past perfect *(PP)*, or past perfect continuous *(PPC)*?

1   I had a dream last night. .....
2   It was about an old house. .....
3   In the dream, I was walking along a corridor. .....
4   I had been there before, many years ago. .....
5   There was an open window and the floor was wet. .....
6   It had been raining earlier. .....
7   But it wasn't raining any more. .....
8   In the dream, I closed the window. .....
9   Then I woke up. .....

2   Past continuous

Neil and Sarah are married and they also work together. This is what they were doing yesterday:

8.00–8.30	having breakfast
8.30–9.15	driving to work
9.15–1.00	working
1.00–2.00	having lunch
2.00–5.00	working
5.00–5.45	driving home
6.30–7.00	having dinner

Make questions and answer them using the examples below.

Neil / 8.15
What was he doing at 8.15?
He was having breakfast.

1 Sarah / 8.40   2 They / 10.30
3 Neil / 1. 15   4 Sarah / 3.00
5 They / 5.30   6 They / 6.45

Then ask a partner what he / she was doing at various exact times yesterday.

3   *when, while, during*

Remember that:

– *when* can go with the past simple and the past continuous
– *while* goes with the past continuous
– *during* goes with a noun or noun phrase.

Choose the correct words.

1   I was eating breakfast (while / when) the post arrived.
2   We had tea (while / during) the meeting.
3   (During / While) I was speaking to him, he was looking out of the window.
4   He worked in a café (while / during) his summer holiday.
5   (When / While) I saw her, she was talking to a tall man with glasses.

4   Past simple and past continuous

Put the verbs in brackets in the correct tense, past simple or past continuous.

I (have) a shower when the doorbell (ring).
I was having a shower when the doorbell rang.

1   I (wrote) a letter when you (phone).
2   They (walk) along the High Street when they (see) the accident.
3   Her friend (take) this photo while she (look) the other way.
4   The plane (fly) at 10,000 metres when the pilot (see) a UFO.
5   While I (live) in London, I (meet) a lot of interesting people.

5   What does it mean?

Choose the correct explanation, A or B.

1   When the singer walked onto the stage, the band were playing her latest hit.
    A The band were in the middle of the song.
    B The band started the song.
2   When the singer walked onto the stage, the band played her latest hit.
    A The band were in the middle of the song.
    B The band started the song.

The past perfect tenses

1 Reporting using the past perfect

When we report things, we use a past tense. Reporting is one of the most frequent uses of the past perfect, because the past perfect is used to report both the past and the present perfect.

She said, 'I've never been to France.'
She said she had never been to France.

He said, 'I've been waiting for an hour.'
He said he had been waiting for an hour.

Report these sentences using the past perfect.

1 He said, 'I've eaten too much!'
2 She said, 'I walked to work.'
3 He said, 'I saw a good film.'
4 She said, 'I've flown on a Boeing 777.'
5 She said, 'I've been working very hard.'
6 She said, 'We weren't listening.'

2 The past perfect

When we are already talking about the past and we want to talk about something that happened earlier, we use the past perfect to make the time clear.

When I arrived the flight had left.
This means that the flight had already gone; it left before the speaker arrived at the airport.

When I arrived the flight left.
This means that the flight didn't leave until the speaker arrived.

Choose the correct words.

1 I didn't see him. When I got there he (went / had gone) home.
2 When I (had done / did) my work I went to bed.
3 After I had finished breakfast, I (went / had gone) for a walk.
4 When I switched on the computer, nothing (had happened / happened) so I called an engineer.
5 By the time I got to the shop, it (closed / had closed) so I couldn't buy any food.

3 The past perfect continuous

The past perfect continuous tells us about a continuous action in the past which began before something else happened. Think of it as the past of the present perfect continuous.

The ground was wet. It had been raining.
This means that the rain had stopped.

The ground was wet. It was raining.
This means that it was still raining.

Choose the correct words.

1 I woke up on the floor. I (was dreaming / had been dreaming) about falling.
2 While she (was typing / had been typing) the computer screen suddenly went black.
3 After we (were playing / had been playing) for an hour, it started snowing.
4 When he (was working / had been working) in London he lived in a small flat.
5 How long (were you waiting / had you been waiting) when she arrived?

4 The past of the past

Last year Anna went back to visit her primary school. It seemed much smaller. Many things had changed. Her old head teacher wasn't there any more.

She had left / retired / moved / died / gone away / become a TV presenter / gone crazy.

Make sentences using the past perfect.

1 Her class teacher, wasn't there any more.
2 The tree in the garden wasn't there any more.
3 There wasn't a canteen any more.
4 Her art teacher, Mr Green, looked completely different.
5 The painting of Bambi wasn't in the hallway any more.
6 The piano wasn't there any more. There was an electronic keyboard instead.

abstract nouns

vocabulary of feelings

Feelings

AND NATALIE IS TOP OF HER CLASS, AND HAS WON THE CUP FOR THE MOST POPULAR STUDENT OF THE YEAR ... AGAIN.

I'VE JUST CRASHED MY CAR

SORRY. I LEFT MY WALLET IN MY OTHER JACKET.

1 What would you say?

What would you say in these situations?

2 Reactions

What reactions were you expressing? Were you expressing more than one reaction? Choose words from the list below.

picture 1:	jealousy, praise, criticism, anger, happiness
picture 2:	sympathy, humour, regret, criticism, relief, anxiety, concern
picture 3:	annoyance, criticism, sarcasm, kindness, boredom, embarrassment

3 Find the adjectives

Match these adjectives with the nouns in **2**, e.g. *jealousy / jealous.*. There is no equivalent adjective for *praise*.

annoyed	angry	anxious	sympathetic
concerned	critical	happy	humorous
regretful	jealous	sarcastic	embarrassed
relieved	kind	bored	

4 Expressing emotion

Say your sentences aloud. Try to communicate the emotion (e.g. jealousy, annoyance) with your voice. The class must guess which emotion you are expressing.

5 The vocabulary of feelings

Draw a table with two columns. Write *positive feelings* at the top of the left hand column, and *negative feelings* at the top of the right hand column. How many words can you write in the columns? Compare lists with a partner.

6 While you're working on this unit ...

During work on this unit put new words for feelings in the two columns. These can be nouns (*anger*), adjectives (*angry*) and adverbs (*angrily*).

Compliments

giving,
accepting and
rejecting
compliments

1 I like your style

What compliments does she give him?
What compliments does he give her?

2 Responding to compliments

You can respond to compliments in two ways. You can accept them with thanks or you can reject them. Listen.

A: Are those new earrings? They really suit you.
B: Oh, thank you. I just got them.

C: I love your jacket.
D: This old thing? I've had it for years.

E: That's a fabulous tie.
F: Thank you. It's my favourite.

G: Lancelot? That's a nice name.
H: Do you like it? I can't stand it.

I: Mm. That was a lovely meal.
J: Thank you.

3 Pair work

You can compliment someone on:
– their name
– their clothes
– their physical appearance
– their possessions
– their achievements or work

Give your partner three compliments. Your partner should respond.

4 Receiving compliments

How do you feel when you receive a compliment?
– Do you believe it?
– Do you feel pleased?
– Do you feel embarrassed?

How do you react when you receive a compliment?
– Do you accept the compliment and thank the person?
– Do you reject the compliment and say something negative?

5 Safe compliments?

Which of these things might you compliment people on?

| men: | tie, name, physique, jacket, car, watch, hair, aftershave, glasses |
| women: | lipstick, hair, clothes, eyes, jewellery, figure, name, perfume |

6 Giving compliments

Go around the class. Give everyone a compliment. Respond to the compliments you receive. Be sincere.

7 Cultural comparison

Compliments on physical appearance are difficult. Women will often compliment other women on their appearance (hair and accessories are the most popular choices), but men should be careful about complimenting women. Some women think such compliments are sexist, i.e. women are being judged on their appearance, not their abilities. The situation is important, too. Compliments may be appropriate at a party which are not appropriate at a business meeting.

The British think it is polite to reject compliments. The Americans give compliments more often and accept them with thanks. In some cultures, any personal comments will cause embarrassment.

Discuss these questions.
– How do you feel about giving and receiving compliments?
– Would you compliment your teacher? Your boss?

Thanks

1 Conversations

 Listen to the conversations. Then practise them using different expressions from the boxes below.

PATIENT Can I see the doctor this morning?

RECEPTIONIST I think she's fully booked. But I'll just check for you.

PATIENT Thanks. I'd appreciate it.

RECEPTIONIST No, I'm sorry. There aren't any free appointments until next week.

PATIENT Oh, dear. Well, thanks anyway. Bye.

RECEPTIONIST Bye.

CUSTOMER I'm trying to find a book. It's called 'Making Your First Million' by Robin Banks.

BOOKSELLER I'll check on the computer for you.

CUSTOMER Thank you.

BOOKSELLER Well, it's not in stock … Maybe we can order it …

CUSTOMER That's very kind of you.

BOOKSELLER Mmm. No, sorry, it's not here. It must be out of print.

CUSTOMER Oh, well. Never mind. Thanks for looking.

BOOKSELLER You're welcome.

Thanking someone	Thanking someone who tries to help (but who does not succeed)	Responding to thanks
Thanks.		You're welcome. (US)
Thank you.		Not at all. (formal, UK)
Thanks a lot.	Thanks anyway.	Don't mention it.
Thank you very much.	Thank you for (looking).	(It's) my pleasure.
It was very kind of you.	Thanks for (trying).	It was nothing.
I appreciate your help.	It doesn't matter. Thanks.	That's alright / OK.
You've been very helpful.	Never mind. Thanks.	No problem.
		Any time.

2 Culture comparison

Most languages have an automatic response to thanks. The British do not automatically respond to thanks, but Americans do. A response is not necessary in British English, but is becoming more frequent. In the past, *You're welcome* sounded very American. Nowadays it's common in Britain too. Remember that *Please* is not an acceptable response to thanks in either Britain or the USA.

conditionals –
type 2

Praise and appreciation

1 Praise

When you comment on someone's work, or on the way someone has done something, you are showing appreciation or giving praise. Can you match the roles with the praise given?

praise given

A Ninety per cent! You've worked very hard.
B Well done, Corporal Jones. We're all very proud of you. You'll get a medal for this.
C You've done very well this month. I'm very pleased with your work.
D Sit! Good boy.
E That's it, Max. Keep your mouth open … wider. Well done. You're doing very well. Good, it's all over … you've been very brave.

role

1 dog owner-dog
2 teacher-student
3 dentist-child patient
4 employer-employee
5 officer-soldier

2 Appreciation

How do you show appreciation? Discuss these situations, then check the answers in section 24 on page 139.

If you were in Britain or the USA, which of the following people would you tip?

☐ I never give gratuities
☐ waiters
☐ hairdressers
☐ hotel porters (UK) / bellhops (US)
☐ taxi drivers
☐ head waiters (UK) / table captains (US)
☐ valets who park your car

How much would you expect to tip a waiter in (a) Britain (b) the USA (c) Spain (d) Japan?

☐ nothing   ☐ 10%   ☐ 20%
☐ a few coins   ☐ 15%   ☐ 25%
☐ 5%   ☐ 17.5%

If you were at a lecture, how would you show your appreciation at the end?

☐ I wouldn't
☐ I'd clap
☐ I'd stand up
☐ I'd shout and cheer
☐ I'd raise my arms in the air
☐ I'd stamp my feet

If you were invited to dinner at a business acquaintance's home in Britain or the USA, what would you take with you?

☐ flowers
☐ chocolates
☐ a bottle of wine
☐ a small gift from my country
☐ business documents
☐ nothing

A foreign business acquaintance has been very helpful to your company. What would you do?

☐ thank them verbally
☐ thank them in a letter
☐ invite them to lunch
☐ give them £500 in an unmarked envelope

See Active Grammar
conditionals – type 2

Criticism

advice
conditionals –
type 2
notes

1 Listen and read

Alex is a laboratory technician at G.L.X. Research plc.

OH, NO, ALEX. YOU'RE DOING IT ALL WRONG! THIS ISN'T GOOD ENOUGH!

SORRY. I'LL TRY AGAIN.

ALEX REACTS WITH A SUBMISSIVE RESPONSE.

SHE'S RIGHT, ALEX. THAT'S COMPLETELY WRONG.

IF YOU'RE SO CLEVER, WHY DON'T YOU DO IT YOURSELF?

ALEX REACTS ANGRILY.

IT'S NOT MY FAULT. NO ONE'S EXPLAINED.

ALEX FEELS HURT. HE THINKS THE CRITICISM IS UNFAIR.

YOU'VE WORKED REALLY HARD ON THIS EXPERIMENT, ALEX. I APPRECIATE THAT.

THANK YOU, MR PATEL.

MR PATEL, THE SUPERVISOR, BEGINS WITH A POSITIVE STATEMENT.

2 Accepting criticism

If someone criticizes you, how should you react? Which of these things should you do? Which shouldn't you do?

– interrupt
– blame someone else
– argue
– accept that it's your fault
– listen carefully
– apologize
– offer to correct the problem
– ask for help
– make sure you understand what's wrong

3 Giving advice

Look at the list in **2** and make sentences.

If I were you, I wouldn't interrupt.
If I were you, I'd apologize.

4 Role-play: Giving positive criticism

Student A is a supervisor at Eurowonderland, an international theme park.

Student B has the job of helping tourists on to the Ghost Train ride. Look at these notes about Student B. Role play the conversation. Student A has to criticize Student B.

Negative	Positive
Didn't greet visitors	Hard-working
Didn't sound polite	Very efficient
Didn't speak clearly	– kept the ride
– difficult to understand	moving
Didn't smile	Very confident
Pushed people into the cars	
Very hot and sweaty	
(no deodorant?)	
Hair untidy	

5 Post role-play

One pair should do their role-play in front of the class, while the rest of the class observe and comment. Was the supervisor as careful as Mr Patel?

When you comment on this role-play you are actually criticizing. How did you do it?

 See Active Grammar
advice; conditionals – type 2

Being a good listener

present perfect
continuous

feel, seem

conditionals –
type 2

1 Conversation

 Listen to this conversation. What is the relationship between the two people? Can you remember some of the things the woman says?

2 Interaction

Student A: turn to this conversation in the Listening appendix. Read A's part. Student B: turn to the Interaction appendix, section 14.

See Active Grammar
present perfect continuous

3 Reflective listening

Reflective listening means that you reflect (or mirror) the emotion that someone is expressing. You do not give advice or opinions. Listen to the recording. You can hear one half of a conversation. Choose the response below which uses reflective listening techniques. Then listen to the recording of the complete conversation.

1 A: Oh, no. What's wrong now?
   B: You sound angry.
2 A: I'm sorry to hear that.
   B: So do I sometimes.
3 A You don't like making coffee.
   B: You don't make it every day.
4 A: Oh, don't get angry about it. It's not important.
   B: So you're worried about your job.
6 A: So? They never thank me either.
   B: So you feel they don't appreciate you.
7 A: In what way?
   B: Yes, you should. I've told you before.
8 A: You think that will make you feel better.
   B: I would if I were you.

4 Menial tasks

The speaker was worried about menial tasks like making the coffee. How would you react if your boss asked you to do one of these tasks?
– empty the waste bin
– buy them something during your lunch break
– change a light bulb
– post a personal letter
– do something else that you don't like

5 Practice

Make a list of things that make you angry, anxious or scared. Tell your partner about them. Your partner should use reflective listening.

6 Using the technique

When do you think this technique might be useful?
– in social conversation
– encouraging someone to talk about a problem
– sympathizing with someone
– interviewing someone
– building a friendship
– helping someone to calm down

See Active Grammar
conditionals – type 2

make
when clauses
after

How often do you get angry?

1 Grading

How strong are these feelings? List these adjectives in order from least angry to most angry.

angry	irritated	annoyed	mad
impatient	furious	tense	

2 Talking about anger

Look at the examples. Make true sentences:

Bad driving	makes	me	tense
Losing a game		him	angry
Personal criticism		her	annoyed
Long queues	make	my friend	furious

I get	angry	when	I lose a game
	impatient		I have to wait
	furious		people drive badly
I lose	my temper		people criticize me

3 Questionnaire

Interview a partner and complete the questionnaire.

1 How many arguments have you had this month?

☐ none
☐ one
☐ less than five
☐ more than five
☐ at least one a day

2 How often do you lose your temper?

☐ never   ☐ rarely
☐ sometimes   ☐ often

3 In which of these places have you complained during the last year?

☐ a restaurant
☐ a bank
☐ at home
☐ a doctor's
☐ a local government office
☐ a shop
☐ a hairdresser's
☐ on the telephone
☐ the post office
☐ school

4 If you complained, did you lose your temper?

☐ yes   ☐ no

5 Did the other person lose their temper?

☐ yes   ☐ no   ☐ I don't think so

6 Did you solve the problem which caused your complaint?

☐ yes   ☐ no   ☐ I don't think so

7 After you had complained, how did you feel?

☐ better   ☐ worse   ☐ the same

8 How do you think the other person felt after you had complained?

☐ superior to you
☐ inferior to you
☐ pleased that the problem had been solved
☐ something else

Complaining

1 Listening

Complaining is a *confrontation* situation.
Listen to the three dialogues.
Which person do you feel sympathetic with in each dialogue?

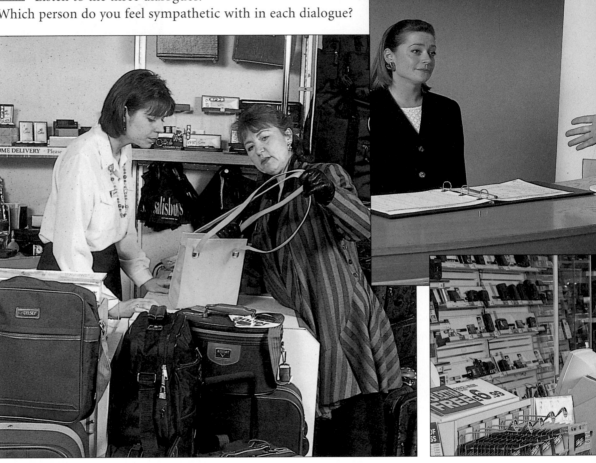

GUEST I want to speak to the manager!

RECEPTIONIST She's not available at the moment. Can I help you?

GUEST I've just checked in and I want to go to my room now. That other receptionist told me I can't. I have to wait till midday!

RECEPTIONIST Well, I'm afraid your room won't be ready until then, because …

GUEST Then you'd better get me another room!

RECEPTIONIST I'm sorry, sir, but we're fully booked and …

GUEST That's your problem. I want my room now!

RECEPTIONIST There's no need to lose your temper, sir.

GUEST Don't you dare speak to me like that!

MANAGER OK, what seems to be the problem?

CUSTOMER I'm sorry about this, but I bought this electric toothbrush from your shop …

MANAGER Uh-huh.

CUSTOMER … and I think it's … um … broken.

MANAGER Did you read the instructions?

CUSTOMER Well, they weren't very clear.

MANAGER Right. Have you got the receipt?

CUSTOMER Well, no. I'm afraid I haven't. I'm sorry.

MANAGER I see.

CUSTOMER Er, can I have my money back?

MANAGER I'm afraid we can't give a refund without a receipt.

CUSTOMER Oh.

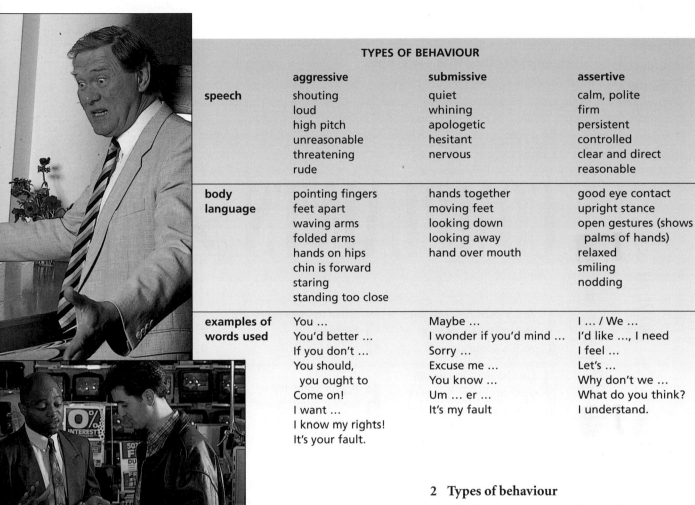

TYPES OF BEHAVIOUR

	aggressive	submissive	assertive
speech	shouting loud high pitch unreasonable threatening rude	quiet whining apologetic hesitant nervous	calm, polite firm persistent controlled clear and direct reasonable
body language	pointing fingers feet apart waving arms folded arms hands on hips chin is forward staring standing too close	hands together moving feet looking down looking away hand over mouth	good eye contact upright stance open gestures (shows palms of hands) relaxed smiling nodding
examples of words used	You … You'd better … If you don't … You should, you ought to Come on! I want … I know my rights! It's your fault.	Maybe … I wonder if you'd mind … Sorry … Excuse me … You know … Um … er … It's my fault	I … / We … I'd like …, I need I feel … Let's … Why don't we … What do you think? I understand.

CUSTOMER Good morning. I'd like a refund for this bag. I bought it last week, and the handle's broken.

ASSISTANT Oh, I'm sorry about that. But we can easily repair it for you.

CUSTOMER I understand that, but I'd prefer a refund.

ASSISTANT Mmm. I see, but we don't usually give refunds … we can repair it now.

CUSTOMER I don't want a repair. I'd like my money back.

ASSISTANT Oh, well, I don't know … you'll have to speak to the manager …

CUSTOMER That's fine. I'll see the manager, then. Thank you.

2 Types of behaviour

The dialogues give examples of three types of behaviour in confrontation situations: *assertive*, *submissive* and *aggressive*. (These words are in the Glossary.)

Look at the chart above and label people in the dialogues with the appropriate types of behaviour.

3 Pair work

Act out the dialogues, using the appropriate voice and body language. Can you continue the conversations?

4 The 'stuck record'

The 'stuck record' is a technique for being assertive. You keep repeating your point politely but firmly. Underline the examples of the technique in the conversation about the bag with a broken handle.

Dealing with complaints

advice
should
let's
must be
would have done
adverbs
conditionals – type 3

1   Ten ways of dealing with complaints

Read the advice.

Dealing with COMPLAINTS

1 You should be calm and relaxed when dealing with a complaint.

2 Let the person explain their problem. If they're angry, let them talk until they've released their anger. Don't interrupt them until they have finished.

3 Never lose your temper. Speak in a friendly, helpful way.

4 Be sympathetic. Use attentive listening techniques. (*I understand, I see.*) Take notes. Use reflective listening techniques. (*You must be very annoyed about this*).

5 Offer to investigate the problem.

6 If your company is wrong, admit it and apologize.

7 Don't waste time defending your company, or blaming someone else. Never make excuses. (*It isn't my fault. We're having problems with the computer system. Someone else was responsible for this.*)

8 Stick to the point. Don't make personal comments. Don't start an argument.

9 Ask the person what they think the answer is.

10 Explain what you're going to do about the problem. Make sure that you do it.

2 Listening

Listen to the telephone conversations, and assess the people who were answering the calls and dealing with the complaints. You can tick more than one box.

	Dialogues			
	one	**two**	**three**	**four**
polite	☐	☐	☐	☐
rude	☐	☐	☐	☐
sympathetic	☐	☐	☐	☐
efficient	☐	☐	☐	☐
aggressive	☐	☐	☐	☐
assertive	☐	☐	☐	☐
submissive	☐	☐	☐	☐

3 Discussion

Listen again. How did the person who was answering deal with the call? Efficiently, sympathetically or politely?

4 What would you have done?

If you had answered the call, would you have ...
– lost your temper?
– listened more sympathetically?
– sounded more helpful?
– transferred the call?
– tried to solve the problem?
– apologized?
– put the phone down?

5 Role-play

Look at the Listening appendix. Choose one of the conversations. Role-play this call with your partner. The situation is the same, but you are answering the call. Deal with the call differently.

See Active Grammar
conditionals – type 3; *would have done;*
adverbs of manner

6 Interaction

You are going to do a role-play. Turn to the Interaction appendix.
Student A: look at section 38.
Student B : look at section 19.

Demonstrate your role-play to the class.

sticking to the
point

avoiding the
issue

Difficult questions

1 Before you listen

Look at the picture. What's happening?
Are these statements true or false?

- People hold press conferences so that they can answer questions.
- During press conferences, people try to answer all the questions fully.
- During press conferences, people avoid answering difficult questions.

2 A political interview

 Listen to the recording. How often does the journalist repeat her question?

3 Sticking to the point

Listen again while looking at the transcript in the Listening appendix. Which of the expressions below does the journalist use when she's sticking to her point?

1 Please answer my question.
2 You still haven't answered my question.
3 Can we get back to my point?

4 Let's stick to the point.
5 But I'd like a direct answer.
6 Don't change the subject.
7 I'm sure we all want an answer to my question.

4 Avoiding the issue

Look again at the transcript. The minister does not give a direct answer to her question at first. He makes several other points instead. What are they? List them.

5 Role-play

The class suggests ideas to complete this question:

Is the government going to …?

Student A is a journalist. Student B is a politician. Role-play the interview, using the new questions.

Present and future time

See Active Grammar

conditionals types 1 – 3

unless

when and future time

1   Present or future?

Choose the correct words.

1   I'll call you when I (will get / get) home from work.
2   I'll get you a drink while you (are waiting / will be waiting).
3   The guide will meet you after you (come / will come) through customs control.
4   When we next visit your country, we (come / will come) to see you.
5   Don't worry, we'll wait until your bus (arrives / will arrive).
6   If it (is / will be) hot tomorrow, we'll go to the beach.
7   I'll change my clothes before I (go / will go) out.
8   Will you wake me up when the film (ends / will end)?

2   Questions

Ask a partner these questions.

What'll you do after you've finished (school / work) tonight?
What'll you do as soon as you get home?
Will you have a (bath / shower) before you have dinner?
Will you watch TV while you're eating?
Will you watch TV after you've finished?
What'll you do before you go to bed?
Will you read before you go to sleep?

3   *if* or *when*?

Complete the spaces with *if* or *when*. Choose the one that seems the most likely.

1   We'll be late ..... we don't hurry.
2   I'll switch on the video ..... the programme begins.
3   I think Liverpool will win the match. I'll be very surprised ..... they don't.
4   I won't be here ..... you arrive. Don't worry, my assistant will look after you.
5   It's OK. ..... you don't have a credit card with you, you can pay by cheque.

4   Conditional – type 1

Put the verbs in brackets in the correct form.

If it (be) wrong you (have to) do it again.
If it is wrong you will have to do it again.

1   You (be) cold if you (not wear) a coat.
2   If I (not feel) well tomorrow, I (not go) to work.
3   If I (not go) to work, my boss (be) angry.
4   If the bus (be) on time, I (be) there at 7.15.
5   You (be) tired tomorrow if you (go) to bed late tonight.
6   If he (have) enough time, he (photocopy) the report for you.

5   Conditionals with modals

Remember that modals like *can, must, may,* and *might* can replace the future simple.

*If it's **nice** tomorrow, I may **go for a long walk**.*
*If you **drive** in America, you **must carry your licence with you**.*
*If you're **thirsty**, I can get you **a cold drink**.*

Rewrite the sentences, replacing the words in bold with other ideas.

6   General truths

When we're talking about general truths, we use the present in both parts of the sentence.

Water freezes when / if the temperature is below zero.
If I eat too much at lunchtime, I always feel tired in the afternoon.
If you mix black and white paint, you get grey.

Make three sentences like this:
–   about a scientific fact
–   about yourself
–   about mixing colours

Conditionals – types 2 and 3

1 Type 1, 2, or 3?

Write *1*, *2*, or *3* next to the sentences below. There are two of each type.

1 If I'm wrong, I'll apologize. .....
2 If I were you, I'd tell him the truth. .....
3 If I'd been in the office, I'd've got your message. .....
4 If I'd known he was new in the job, I wouldn't have been so annoyed. .....
5 If you call Directory Enquiries, they'll give you the number. .....
6 I would buy a new car if I had enough money. .....

Which of these sentences are about past time? Write *P* next to them.

2 Type 2 conditionals

Write full answers to these questions:

1 What would you do if you won a lot of money?
   If I won a lot of money, I'd ...
2 Where would you go if you could go anywhere in the world?
3 If you could have dinner with anyone in the world, who would you choose?
4 If you could be someone else, who would you like to be?

3 *If I were you …*

Choose the correct verbs.

1 If I were you, I (won't / wouldn't) drive so fast.
2 Which one (will / would) you buy if you were me?
3 If I (am / were) you, I ('ll /'d) take more exercise.
4 If Anna were here, she (would / had) help us, but unfortunately she isn't.

4 Type 1 and type 2

Sometimes it's easy to decide whether to use a type 1 or type 2 conditional. Sometimes it's your opinion. Do you think something is very unlikely or impossible? Or do you think it's a possibility?

I might meet Mrs Smith, a business colleague, this afternoon. It's possible.
If I meet her, I'll shake hands. (type 1) BUT
If I met the Queen of Denmark, I'd shake hands. (type 2)

Choose the verbs – remember it's your opinion of probability, not a question of grammar.

1 If I (have / had) any homework tonight, I ('ll /'d) do it after dinner.
2 I (won't / wouldn't) tell anyone if I (fail / failed) my exams.
3 If it (rains / rained) tomorrow, I ('ll /'d) take an umbrella.

5 Type 3 conditionals (1)

These are also called past conditionals. Choose the correct verbs.

1 If I (would / had) known she was ill, I (would / will) have visited her in hospital.
2 If he'd (get / got) up earlier, he (wouldn't / won't) have been late for work.
3 I would (have helped / helped) you if I (was / had been) there.
4 If I'd (remember / remembered) your phone number, I ('ll /'d) have called you.
5 Sorry, if I'd (knew / known) you were asleep, I wouldn't have (turn / turned) on my CD player.

6 Type 3 conditionals (2)

Complete the sentences.

If I'd been born one hundred years ago …
… I'd've been in the First World War.
… I could have met Charlie Chaplin.

1 If I'd lived in the nineteenth century …
2 If I'd been born in England …
3 If I hadn't started learning English …

Rumour and gossip

Looking for the truth

deductions
whether

1 Tell the story

Tell the story of the pictures to your partner. Ask questions about the characters, where they are, what time it is and what happens. Then change partners and compare stories. Use the words below.

A: *Who's Mr Marriot?*
B: *I think he's the … / He must be the … / He's probably … / He could be …*
A: *What's wrong with Myrtle?*
B: *Perhaps she fainted / She may have fainted.*

managing director	to overhear something
boss	to gossip
manager	to have a tea-break
secretary	to start a rumour
messenger	fainted
clerk	fallen over the tea trolley
typist	been hit over the head
receptionist	had a heart attack
computer operator	
tea lady	

2 After you've told the story

Did you say …
– how many vending machines Mr Marriot mentioned?
– how many vending machines the messenger mentioned?
– whether the messenger was reporting a fact or starting a rumour?
– why Myrtle was on the floor?
– whether she was really going to lose her job or not?

If you didn't do these things, do them now.

3 The rumour

There are some facts in the story. People made deductions from the facts.
Complete the spaces below:

Mr Marriot mentioned .....^{1} vending ......^{2} The .....^{3} overheard him. When he reported this, he changed vending machine from singular to .....^{4}. When the other workers heard the .....^{5}, they were worried. They thought that the vending machines would replace the .....^{6}, and the tea ladies would lose their ......^{7}.

4 Language and gender

People try not to use *gender-marked* words in business. A gender-marked word is one which tells us the sex of the person who does the job, e.g. *policeman*. A word which can describe either sex is an *inclusive* word, e.g. *police officer*.

There was a gender-marked job title in the story. What was it? (There isn't a well-known inclusive alternative.)

5 Matching

On the left are some gender-marked job titles. On the right are some inclusive job titles which have replaced them. Match the job titles.

gender-marked job titles	inclusive job titles
air hostess / steward	server
actor, actress	technician, engineer
waiter, waitress	chairperson
cameraman	flight attendant
repair man	actor
fireman	messenger
salesman / woman	nurse
foreman	salesperson
chairman / woman	fire fighter
male nurse	executive
businessman / woman	supervisor
post-boy	camera operator

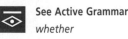

See Active Grammar
whether

120

Facts, deduction, speculation

could be

could have done

past perfect continuous

deduction and speculation

1 Listening

 Listen to Jeff and Jim talking later the same day about the incident with Myrtle. Are these sentences true (✓) or false (✗)?

1 Someone told Myrtle she had lost her job. .....
2 Myrtle knew this already. .....
3 Myrtle had been working there for fifteen years. .....
4 The messenger had been reading Mr Marriot's letters. .....
5 The messenger had heard Mr Marriot talking to his secretary. .....
6 Mr Marriot said he wasn't expecting any vending machines. .....
7 Mr Marriot said he was going to put vending machines in the factory. .....

---

deduction /dɪˈdʌkʃn/ noun [C,U] 1 something that you work out from facts that you already know; the skill of reasoning in this way
It was a brilliant piece of deduction by the detective.
jump to conclusions to decide that something is true without thinking about it carefully enough.
speculate /ˈspekjʊleɪt/ verb 1 [I,T] speculate (about/on sth) to think about sth without having all the facts or information
to speculate about the result of the next election
speculation /ˌspekjʊˈleɪʃn/ noun [C,U] an act of speculating

---

2 Definitions

Read the definitions and listen again. Which of these things were Jeff and Jim doing during their conversation?
– making deductions
– reporting facts
– speculating
– jumping to conclusions

 See Active Grammar
past perfect continuous; deduction and speculation

3 Deduction v speculation

Imagine you're working for the company. Use the tables in the Active Grammar appendix and make sentences about these statements.

Jim is very upset about Myrtle.
He must know her well.
He might be her husband.

Myrtle received a huge bunch of flowers after her accident.
They must have been expensive.
Her co-workers might have bought them.
Mr Marriot could have sent them.

1 Mr Marriot has a big office and wears expensive suits.
2 Sharon takes phone messages for Mr Marriot.
3 Mr Marriot was late for work this morning.
4 Myrtle has a bandage round her forehead.
5 Everyone in the factory is angry.

Changing times

reason:
because,
because of

vocabulary:
employment

think, reckon,
guess

1 True or false?

Are these statements true or false for
your country?

..... Unemployment has risen in recent
years.
..... Jobs have been created in new industries.
..... Traditional jobs have been lost.
..... Many people have been made redundant in my town.
..... Machines are replacing people.
..... Unemployment is highest among young people.
..... Older people who lose their jobs find it difficult to get new ones.

2 Matching

Find the best endings for the *result* sentences. Use the link words
because or *because of*. Which phrases in the *reason* column contain a verb?

result	link word	reason
1 Tea ladies have lost their jobs...	because	A tourism.
2 People will study for more years...	because of	B job losses.
3 Small farms are disappearing...		C vending machines.
4 People can work from home...		D they can use computers and modems.
5 People have more leisure time...		E automation.
6 Jobs have been created...		F they aren't as efficient as large ones.
7 Workers may go on strike...		G they won't be able to find jobs.

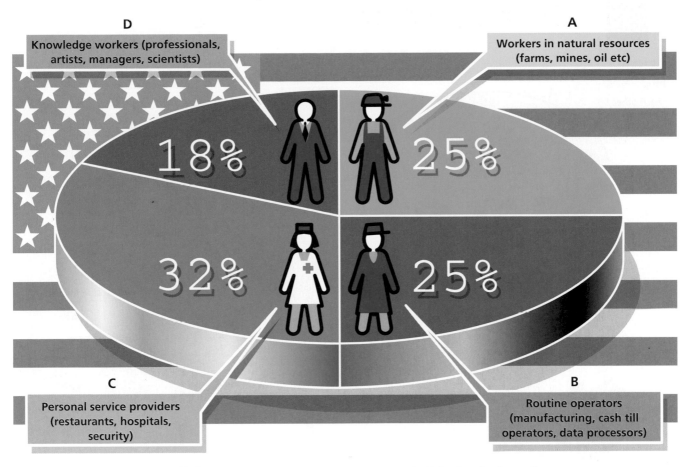

D
Knowledge workers (professionals, artists, managers, scientists)

A
Workers in natural resources (farms, mines, oil etc)

18% 25%

32% 25%

C
Personal service providers (restaurants, hospitals, security)

B
Routine operators (manufacturing, cash till operators, data processors)

3 Types of job

The diagram shows different divisions in the American workforce today.

Which divisions would you put these jobs into? Discuss with a partner.

..... computer operators
..... bank clerks
..... designers
..... secretaries
..... catering workers (e.g. waiters, cooks)
..... government workers
..... domestic workers (e.g. cleaners)
..... teachers
..... managers
..... farm workers
..... shop assistants
..... workers in manufacturing
..... healthcare workers (e.g. nurses)
..... workers in leisure and sport
..... miners
..... military personnel (e.g. soldiers)
..... police officers
..... lawyers
..... tour guides

4 Jobs for the future?

What kind of jobs will there be in the future? Look at the list of occupations. Work with a partner.

Put a tick (✔) if you think more jobs will be created.
Put a cross (✘) if you think jobs will be lost.
Put an equals sign (=) if you think the number of jobs in this area will be about the same.

Now turn to the chart in expressing opinions in the Active Grammar appendix. Using the chart, discuss your answers with the class.

 See Active Grammar
expressing opinions

Understanding each other

clarification

paraphrasing

*each other /
one another*

1 Before you listen

Ms Hardie is a trade union official. She has
made an appointment to see Mr Marriot.
Look at the five pictures of their conversation.
Read the descriptions of their body language
and match them with the pictures.

A Mr Marriot is showing the palms of his
   hands.
B Mr Marriot is leaning back. Ms Hardie is
   standing, with files in front of her as a
   barrier.
C Mr Marriot and Ms Hardie are mirroring
   each other's body language.
D Ms Hardie has folded her arms across her
   chest and is sitting up straight.
E Mr Marriot is leaning forward and
   pointing his pen at Ms Hardie.

2 What do these gestures show?

Which gestures demonstrate these feelings?
– feeling superior
– feeling unsure and tense
– trying to show you're being honest
– being aggressive
– feeling 'I am right. You are wrong.'
– coming to an agreement

3 Listen and match

 Listen, and match the sentences with
the pictures.

A *We're not going to allow it.*
B *Now wait a minute, Ms Hardie …*
C *Let me get this straight …*
D *Please take a seat.*
E *I don't understand. Where did you hear
   that?*

4 Find words which mean …

Look in the Listening appendix and find words and phrases which mean:

1 worried and unhappy
2 make sure I understand this completely
3 tell someone they can no longer work for the company
4 put in (a piece of equipment)
5 asked anyone for their opinion
6 solved the problem

Look at this example:
1 *worried and unhappy*

Transcript: The tea ladies are *very upset* about losing their jobs.
Paraphrase: The tea ladies are *worried and unhappy* about losing their jobs.

Find the sentences in the transcript which 2-6 come from. Paraphrase them.

5 Paraphrasing

There are two examples of paraphrasing in the conversation.

You're telling me that I'm going to sack the tea ladies and install vending machines all over the building.

You're saying that you're not going to sack the tea ladies, and you're only installing one vending machine.

Which expressions introduce the paraphrases?

 See Active Grammar
each other / one another

Paraphrasing

1 Introducing paraphrasing

Paraphrasing means repeating things in a different way. You use the technique to:
- check that you have understood what someone means.
- emphasize a point, or make sure that your meaning is clear. This is useful when speaking to people whose first language is not English.

> **Introducing paraphrasing**
> So you mean …
> What you mean is …
> What you're saying is …
> Let me get this clear …
> Let me get this straight …

2 The systems consultant

Mr Marriot is speaking to Daniel Elgin, a systems consultant. He wants Daniel to find out some information for him.
Role-play Daniel, and paraphrase Mr Marriot's sentences using the formulas in the box. You can add other information if you know it.

1 'Daniel, I need some facts and figures about vending machines. You know, cost of monthly rentals and so on.'
2 'I'd like to know how many we would need for the offices and the factory.'
3 'I also want to know how much tea ladies are costing us, including wages and national insurance.'
4 'Talk to the staff, do a questionnaire or something. See how they feel about tea ladies and whether they'd miss them.'
5 'Make sure your survey emphasizes the positive advantages of vending machines, you know what I mean?'
6 'And I want a copy of our agreement with the trade union. Does it say anything about consultation?'

preferences

The answers you want

1 The survey

Mr Marriot wanted a survey which 'emphasizes the positive advantages of vending machines.' Daniel thought of ten questions. He only used five of them for the questionnaire. The ten questions are below. Which five did he use?

2 Pair work

Student A: ask Student B Daniel's five questions.
Student B: ask Student A the other five questions.

Our present service offers tea or coffee in the morning, and tea in the afternoon. Would you prefer more choice?
☐ Yes ☐ No

Do you like the taste of tea and coffee from vending machines?
☐ Yes ☐ No

Would you like to have a choice of ice cold drinks as well as hot drinks?
☐ Yes ☐ No

Do changes in your daily routine make you feel uncomfortable?
☐ Yes ☐ No

Do you prefer friendly personal service to machines?
☐ Yes ☐ No

Is the tea from the tea trolleys always fresh and hot?
☐ Yes ☐ No

Are you happy with the present system?
☐ Yes ☐ No

Would you like to have hot drinks whenever you want, or do you prefer just twice a day?
☐ Yes ☐ No

Do you prefer tea and coffee which has just been made?
☐ Yes ☐ No

Do you prefer having hot drinks while you're working, or do you prefer stopping work and taking a proper break?
☐ drinks while I'm working
☐ taking a break

Consequences

conditionals –
types 1 and 2

consequences

because

1 The report

Daniel wrote a report for Mr Marriot. Daniel was very formal. He used long words instead of short words and he didn't use contractions. This is a section of the report. Find words which mean:

1 tea ladies
2 to work for
3 holiday or vacation
4 to do her or his work
5 the places where the tea ladies stop
6 drinks
7 to stop

Beverage service operatives and service locations

At present, five beverage service operatives are employed by the company. If one operative is sick or absent on annual leave, the others have to perform her or his tasks. When this happens, each operative has 25% more work. Consequently, their 'rounds' take longer. If they take longer, they arrive later at the majority of service locations. If employees normally have beverages at (e.g.) eleven, they will cease work at that time and wait. If the operative is fifteen minutes late, employees will wait and talk, then will still take their normal break when beverages arrive.

Each operative has three weeks paid annual leave per year, so for fifteen weeks per year there will only be four operatives. If someone is sick during the fifteen weeks of annual leave, there will only be three operatives. As a result, they will arrive much later at service locations.

2 Paraphrase the report

Can you paraphrase the argument in his report in more informal language?

3 Sharon's argument

Daniel gave the report to Sharon. Sharon didn't agree with his conclusion. This is Sharon's argument. Complete the spaces:

1 'If we decided on vending machines, we ..... only afford to rent five or six machines for the same cost as the tea ladies' service.'
2 'If we had vending machines we ..... not be able to have them in every office.'
3 'Machines aren't perfect. They break down, and they run out of tea, coffee, milk or sugar. If the nearest machine broke down, people ..... have to go to the next machine.'
4 'If they ..... to go to a machine on another floor, they would waste time.'
5 'If they walked through another office, they ..... stop and talk to people on the way.'
6 'If this happened, they ..... waste other people's time as well as their own.'

 See Active Grammar
conditionals – types 1 & 2

4 Discuss

Who do you agree with? Daniel or Sharon? Why?

I agree / disagree with (Daniel) because …
I think (Sharon) is right because …

reason
result
for and *against*

Reasons and results

1 The Acme Water Cooler

Daniel discovered that Acme Vending Machines could also supply water coolers. There was a choice of either containers with flat bases (cups) or containers with pointed bases (cones). He called Acme and asked for their advice.

Complete the spaces with reason and result words from the box.

reason	result
because	therefore
because of	so that
	as a result

'We advise cones for one reason. .....[1] people often do not finish their drinks, they put cups down on a desk or other surface. These often get knocked over and .....[2] water spills onto documents, or worse, into computer equipment. They also forget about them and leave them around, ...[3] offices become untidy and full of litter. If people are using cones, they cannot put them down .....[4] the pointed ends. .....[5] they have to hold them while they're having a drink. .....[6] this, people put less water into a cone. They know they will have to finish the contents before they can dispose of the cone. .....[7], you'll save on water, the office will be tidier and you won't have spilled drinks.'

2 Cones v cups

Disagree with Daniel.
Give reasons why cones are a bad idea.
Give reasons why cups are a good idea.

3 For and against

Work in groups. Choose one of the topics below and give reasons *for* and *against* each thing or idea.
– pencils versus pens
– reference books versus CD-Roms
– microwave ovens versus conventional ovens
– real fur versus synthetic fur
– petrol versus diesel fuel
– sitting in a circle in class versus sitting in rows in class

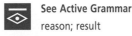

See Active Grammar
reason; result

Expressing opinions

argument

contrast
(however)

based on

1 Listening

 Listen to the six opinions and answer the questions. You may want to read the questions first and check any problem words in the Glossary.

See Active Grammar
contrast (however)

2 The committee

Work in groups of three. You are going to discuss the question of vending machines. Turn to the Interaction appendix.

Student A (for): look at section 10
Student B (against): look at section 26.
Student C (compromise): look at section 21.

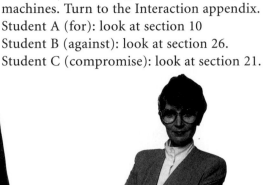

JIM HEWITT, factory worker

Which person does he think has shown more loyalty to the company, Myrtle Hewitt or Alistair Marriot?
What does he mean by 'loyalty'?
Is he being aggressive or assertive?
Can you demonstrate his body language for these sentences?
'There'll be trouble on the factory floor. And that'll cost you!'

SHARON MAXWELL, Personal Assistant to the Managing Director

Does she take sides in the argument or does she 'sit on the fence'?
What is her suggestion for a compromise?

ROZ HARDIE, Trade union representative for the area

What important point does she make about the survey?
Does she discuss the question of vending machines versus tea ladies?
What is her main point?

ALISTAIR MARRIOT, Managing Director

What is his main worry?
In your opinion, is he for or against vending machines?
Is your opinion based on facts or feelings?
What does he intend to do?

MYRTLE HEWITT, tea lady

Does Myrtle talk about her feelings or about the facts?
What can she do that a machine can't?
In your opinion, is this important?

DANIEL ELGIN, Systems Consultant

Is his argument based on facts or emotions?
What facts does he use in his argument?
What is his conclusion?

Talking about the present

See Active Grammar

deduction and speculation

may, might

would have done

See also Language Focus 4

possibility and certainty

1 Guess the word

This is a guessing game which uses deduction. You have to guess which word from the box your partner is thinking of. You can ask only direct *yes/no* questions.

an orange	the moon	a dog
an electrician	an apple	a bird
a secretary	a lemon	a cat
a footballer	a spider	a star
a banana	a plane	a car
a cassette	the sun	

First practise. Complete the spaces with *must, could, might,* or *can't.*

A: Is it a person?

B: No, it isn't.

A: So, it ..... be a secretary. Is it an animal?

B: No, it isn't.

A: So it ..... be a cat. Is it in the sky?

B: Yes, it is.

A: So it ..... be the sun, it ..... be a plane, it ..... be a star, it ..... the moon. Can you see it during the day?

B: No, you can't.

A: So, it ..... be the sun, or a plane. Can you see it at night?

B: Yes, you can.

A: So, it could be the moon or it ..... be a star. Is it the moon?

B: No, it isn't.

A: OK. It ..... be a star.

2 Which questions?

Which of these other questions might be useful for playing the game? Put a tick.

..... Is it round?

..... Is it square?

..... Is it yellow?

..... Is it blue?

..... Is it a machine?

..... Do they work with their hands?

..... Do they work indoors?

..... Can they type?

..... Can it fly?

..... Can it swim?

..... Can you sit inside it?

..... Is there one in this room?

..... Can you eat it?

..... Does it have four legs?

..... Can you drink it?

..... Has it got wheels?

3 Play the game

Try the game with a partner.

Then try the game with some other words.

4 *so, because, because of*

Complete the spaces with *so, because,* or *because of.*

1 It's made of gold ..... it must be expensive.

2 He must be tired ..... he went to bed very late last night.

3 I know that the fish can't be fresh ..... its terrible smell!

4 I may be late ..... the heavy traffic.

5 It can't be hers. It's too small, ... it must be his.

5 Responses

Look at the statements and match them with the responses.

Statements

1 I've been driving all day.

2 I've been standing in a queue for an hour.

3 I get terrible marks in all my tests.

4 I'm going to make a record with Madonna.

5 I've got a very high temperature.

6 I've been to the moon on a UFO.

7 I'm on holiday in the Sahara Desert.

Responses

You must be joking! A

You can't be telling the truth. B

You must feel terrible. C

You must be exhausted. D

You can't be revising enough. E

It must be very hot. F

You must be getting annoyed. G

131

Talking about the past

1 *must have been* – expressing empathy

Match the statements with the responses.

Statements

1 I broke my arm last year.
2 I woke up and found a burglar in my room.
3 I had to work for 72 hours last week.
4 I was in Alaska last winter.
5 I met the Prince of Wales last month.

Responses

You must have been pretty tired.   A
You must have been very excited.   B
It must have been painful.   C
You must have been really scared.   D
It must have been very cold.   E

2 Perfect forms (1)

Complete the sentences using *must have (done)*, *can't have (done)*, or *might have (done)*.

Did he see it?
Yes, he must have seen it.
No, he can't have seen it.
I don't know. He might have seen it.

1 Did she know? No, …
2 Did he meet her? I don't know, …
3 Did they understand? Yes, …
4 Was she angry? Yes, …
5 Have they finished? No, …
6 Has he heard the news? I don't know, …

3 Perfect forms (2)

Write sentences as in the example.

She had a bad skiing accident. Fortunately she was all right, but (she / could / kill herself).
She could have killed herself

1 'I can't find my textbook.' 'You (must / leave / it at home).'
2 'I phoned you, but there was no answer.' 'Really? I (may / be / in the shower).'
3 'The driver didn't stop.' 'He (can't / see / the traffic signal).'
4 'He was supposed to meet us at six.' 'He (must / forget).'

5 'That was stupid. You (could / hurt / yourself).'
6 'She got 99% in the exam.' 'It (can't / be / very difficult).'

4 *(might) do / might (have done)*, etc.

Write sentences using the word in brackets.

Perhaps she'll be at the party. (might)
She might be at the party.

I expected to see her, but she wasn't there. Perhaps she stayed at home. (might)
She might have stayed at home.

1 We'll probably be there at two o'clock. (should)
2 We expected them here at ten, but they didn't arrive. (should)
3 His story was impossible. He wasn't telling the truth, I'm sure. (can't)
4 That's not correct. I'm certain. (can't)
5 The bus usually leaves at nine. It's ten past and we've just arrived at the bus stop. We're sure that it's already left. (must)
6 It's correct, I'm sure. (must)
7 Maybe we'll hear good news tomorrow. (may)
8 She wasn't here yesterday. Perhaps she was ill. (may)
9 I don't know who did it. Perhaps it was him. (could)

5 Deduction and speculation

Choose the best words to complete the sentences.

1 It can't (has / have) been a UFO. That's (possible / impossible).
2 It must (be / been) right. The computer couldn't have (make / made) a mistake.
3 Take a coat. It looks sunny outside, but it (might / can't) be cold.
4 You were very lucky. You (must / could) have (injure / injured) yourself badly.
5 That's funny. She's late. Perhaps she (missed / must have missed) the bus.

Interaction appendix

SECTION 1 *(page 98)*
Student D

This is your basic story. Try to add details. The words in (brackets) should help you.

A long-distance truck driver stopped for a meal (*where? when?*). The driver was eating and drinking (*what?*) when some young men from a motor-cycle gang (*how many? describe them*) came in and started causing trouble (*how?*). They drank the driver's drink (*what?*) and ate some of his food (*what?*). The driver did nothing. He got up, paid the bill and left. One of the young men spoke to the café owner. 'That driver isn't much of a man,' he said. The owner was looking out of the window and replied, 'He isn't much of a driver either. He's just driven his truck over some (*how many?*) motorcycles.'

SECTION 2 *(page 81)*
Student A

Role-play 1: You have the good news. Speak first.

You are a recently appointed sales representative for Acme Vacuum Cleaners. You are going to see your boss, the sales director. This is your first month with the company and you have some great news. You have just sold 10,000 vacuum cleaners to Worldwide Hotels plc. This means you have sold more than any of the other representatives this month. You think they'll buy more next year.

Role-play 2: You have the bad news. Let your partner speak first.

A member of your family has an old car. They are very proud of it. They use it only at weekends. They've often told you that it is valuable, but you don't think this is true. Today your car broke down and you had an important appointment. You needed a car, so you borrowed the old car. You didn't ask permission. There was no time. You've never driven it before. On the way home you had to stop suddenly. The old car's brakes are not as good as modern ones, and you crashed into a wall. You are fine, but the car is damaged. You have to tell the family member (the owner of the old car) the bad news. Offer to pay for the damage.

SECTION 3 *(page 11)*
Student A

Work in pairs. You are going to do two role-plays.

Role-play 1: Ordering a meal

You are in a restaurant with your friends, James and Anna. Order a meal from Student B. Student B is going to write down your order. On the menu there are notes. J = James, A = Anna, Y = you.

MENU
APRIL 12th

Starter
Tomato soup J
Orange juice A
Fried mushrooms Y

Main Course
Chicken & chips Y
Pizza A
Spaghetti Bolognese J

Dessert
Chocolate ice-cream J
Chocolate cake A
Danish pastry Y

Role-play 2: Taking the order

Student B is going to order a meal. Write down their order. Then deliver the meal to them.

SECTION 4 *(page 67)*
Student A

You're going to have a telephone conversation with Student B. Your half of the conversation is in the box below. Read it first, and put slashes (/) where you think Student B is going to speak.

Then act out the conversation with Student B.

> 28492. Hi, *(use B's real name)*. I'd love to, but which day is it? What time? In the evening? Oh, dear. I'm afraid I can't. I'm sorry, but I have to get up early on Sunday. I'm taking my mother to the airport. I'm terribly sorry, *(use B's real name)*. Oh, yes, I'd love to. Yes, sorry again. See you. Bye.

SECTION 5 *(page 36)*
Listeners

There are three listeners. You are each going to listen to someone speaking in a conversation. Reply if you are asked questions. Nod and smile and make agreeing noises if you like.

Student 1

You are going to avoid eye contact. Don't look directly at the speaker. Look away, look past them, look down – but do not look them in the eyes!

Student 2

You are going to listen with great attention. Try to keep eye contact with the speaker as much as you can.

Student 3

You can do what you want. Just sit back and listen to the speaker in your normal way.

SECTION 6 *(page 49)*
Student A

You are going to role-play two telephone conversations. In each conversation you are going to exchange facts on the telephone. You will need to note the facts.

Role-play 1: Caller

You are calling a travel agent and booking a British Airways flight from London to Paris.

– You want an afternoon flight next Saturday, to arrive in Paris before 6 p.m.
– You prefer to fly from Heathrow airport, but Gatwick airport is also possible.
– You will need to give your name, address and a telephone number.
– You will need to know, the flight number, the time it departs from London, and the time it arrives in Paris.
– You are paying for the flight with a Passport credit card, number 4459-0031-1660-9019, expiry date July next year. You will need to know the price of the ticket.

Role-play 2: Travel agent

You are a travel agent for Winton Travel. Student B is calling you to book their car onto the Channel Tunnel train. You need to know these facts:

– the caller's name, address and a telephone number
– the date they want to travel (and what day of the week it is, if they are travelling between 14 July and 4 September)
– the registration number and make of their car
– how they want to pay
– if they're paying by credit card, the type, number and expiry date
– where to send the ticket

Here is a price list:
Please note: the prices in the table are for the purpose of practising your English only. For real prices, contact a travel agent!

FOLKESTONE – CALAIS		
Channel Tunnel trains		
dates	times	price per car
1 Jan - 30 Apr	every 30 mins	£43
1 May - 13 Jul	every 20 mins	£59
14 Jul - 4 Sep Fri/ Sat	every 15 mins	£123
14 Jul - 4 Sep Sun - Thur	every 15 mins	£91
3 - 30 Sep	every 20 mins	£59
1 Oct - 31 Dec	every 30 mins	£51
Journey time: 35 minutes Maximum car height: 1.85 metres		

SECTION 7 *(page 98)*
Student A

This is your basic story. Try to add details. The words in (brackets) should help you.

Someone (*who? when?*) was having a meal at a very famous hotel (*which hotel? where?*). They had the hotel's special cake for dessert (*describe it*). They liked it very much, and sent a note to the kitchen. They asked the chef for the recipe. They received the recipe, plus a bill for the recipe, which was a lot of money (*how much?*). They asked a lawyer about it. The lawyer said they had to pay. Now the person publicizes the special recipe everywhere (*how?*).

SECTION 8 *(page 36)*
Student C

This is your reading text. Think about where you are going to pause. Then try reading to the rest of the class. Try to make eye contact with as many people as you can while you're reading.

> Eyes are important. Look at some toy animals – and at Disney cartoon characters like Bambi. They always have huge eyes. We feel good when we see things with large eyes, because they look like human babies. For this reason, the good characters in cartoons have large eyes, and the bad characters have small eyes.

SECTION 9 *(page 24)*
Student A

You are going to do two role-plays.

Role-play 1: At the railway station

Student B is meeting you and a friend at a railway station in London. You and your friend are going to do an English language course in London. Student B is going to greet you, and start a conversation. Here is some information.

Journey:	The train was very slow. It was full. There were no seats.
Weather:	It was very hot in your country. It's cold here!
Visits:	This is your first visit, but your friend was here last year.
Job /Place of study:	Tell the truth
Your home:	Tell the truth
Plans:	You're going to be here for four weeks.
Hotel:	You aren't going to stay in a hotel. You are going to stay with an English family.

Role-play 2: At the airport

You are meeting Student B at an airport in your country. Student B is visiting your country on business. Greet Student B. Introduce yourself and start a conversation.

SECTION 10 *(page 130)*
Student A

Some arguments *for* vending machines:

– Cost. Vending machines are cheaper. The monthly rental is low, and all maintenance is done by Acme Vending Machines. Therefore the company doesn't have to do anything.
– The machines work 24 hours a day, so employees can buy drinks whenever they want.
– Tea trolleys are noisy and interrupt work. The tea break is a social occasion because everyone stops at the same time.
– Employees can have drinks while they work, and will not need to stop for official breaks.
– The tea ladies use a kitchen on the first floor. This must be checked by Health and Safety officers at regular intervals.
– Cups and saucers have to be washed up. Vending machines use disposable cups.

See also Daniels's report (page 128) on the disadvantages of tea ladies.

SECTION 11 *(page 53)*
Student B

You are going to do two role-plays.

Role-play 1: Applicant

You are the applicant. Answer the interviewer's questions, and ask these questions about the job.

How much will I earn?
Will I have to work on Sundays?
Is there medical insurance with the job?
Can I have my annual holidays during August?

Role-play 2: Interviewer

You are the interviewer. Ask questions about the applicant's résumé, plus these extra questions.

What was your journey like?
Was our address easy to find?
Tell me about your last job.
Tell me about your family.
What subjects were your worst at school?
Why was that?
Why do you want this job?

SECTION 12 *(page 70)*

Here are the scores for the personality test:

1	A 1	B 0	C 2	5	A 1	B 0	C 2
2	A 2	B 0	C 1	6	A 0	B 2	C 1
3	A 1	B 2	C 0	7	A 0	B 1	C 2
4	A 2	B 0	C 1	8	A 2	B 1	C 0

Add up your score then look at section 18 below to see what your score means.

SECTION 13 *(page 49)*
Student B

You are going to role-play two telephone conversations. In each conversation you are exchanging facts on the telephone. You will need to note the facts.

Role-play 1: Travel agent

You are a travel agent, and you work for Apex Travel. Student A is telephoning you to book a British Airways flight to Paris. You have a timetable below. Remember that Paris time is one hour later than London time, and that there are flights from two airports. You will need to know these facts:

– the traveller's name
– where they want to go
– the airport they want to fly from
– a telephone number and address
– how they are going to pay (the ticket costs £295)
– if they're paying by credit card, you need to know the type of card, the number and the expiry date
– where they want you to send the ticket

TIMETABLE
London-Paris (Charles de Gaulle)

days	depart	from	arrive	flight no.
1234567	12.30	LHR-4	14.35	BA314
1234567	13.30	LGW-N	15.30	BA2832
1234567	14.15	LHR-4	16.20	BA316
12345-7	15.30	LGW-N	17.30	BA2836
12345-7	16.00	LHR-4	18.05	BA318
1234567	17.15	LHR-4	19.20	BA322

Airport information: LHR - London Heathrow,
LGW - London Gatwick
Terminal numbers: 4 = LHR terminal 4,
N = LGW North terminal
Days: 1 = Monday, 2 = Tuesday etc.

Role-play 2: Caller

You are calling Student B. You want to book your car with two passengers onto the Channel Tunnel train from England to France. You want to know:

– how long the journey is
– how often the trains go
– how much the ticket is

You will need to give these facts:

– your name, address and telephone number
– the date when you are travelling (and what day of the week this is)
– the number of passengers
– the registration number of your car (P659 HRU)
– the make and model of your car (Ford Escort)
– your Passport credit card number 6165-9505-3954-2817, expiry date October next year

SECTION 14 *(page 110)*
Student B

Student A is going to read from the Listening appendix. Respond to A. The sentences below will help you. You needn't use them all.

I'm sorry to hear (that).
You look / sound (worried).
You must feel (anxious).
It seems as if (she doesn't appreciate you).
How do you feel about (that)?
In what way?
Can you give me an example?

SECTION 15 *(page 67)*
Student B

You're going to have a telephone conversation with Student A. Your half of the conversation is in the box below. Read it first, and put slashes (/) where you think Student A is going to speak. Then act out the conversation with Student A.

Hello, (use A's real name). It's (use your name). I'm having a party next week. Would you like to come? On Saturday. Ten o'clock. Yes. Oh, no! Oh, I see. Another time, perhaps? Great. See you soon. Bye.

SECTION 16 *(page 98)*
Student B

This is your basic story. Try to add details. The words in (brackets) should help you.

Someone (*who?*) was in a shop (*which shop? where? when?*). They were looking at some merchandise (*what?*) which had come from a tropical country (*which country?*). Suddenly the person fell over (*did anything else happen?*). People (*who?*) rushed over, and called an ambulance. The hospital said that something poisonous (*what? a snake? a spider? a scorpion?*) had bitten the person. The shop examined the merchandise and found some of the poisonous things (*how many? was the person all right in the end?*).

SECTION 17 *(page 24)*
Student B

You are going to do two role-plays.

Role-play 1: At the railway station.

You are meeting Student A at a railway station in London. Student A is visiting London with a friend. They are going to study English. You are a guide from the language school. Greet them. Introduce yourself and start a conversation.

Role-play 2: At the airport

You are visiting Student A's country on business. You are from Australia. Student A is going to greet you at the airport. Here is some information.

Journey:	The flight was very long, but you had excellent meals on the plane. You are tired.
Weather:	It was very nice in Australia. You were on the beach yesterday.
Visits:	This is your third visit. You like Student A's country very much.
Job:	You work for Australian Children's TV. You're a TV journalist.
Your home:	You live in Bathurst. It's near Sydney.
Plans:	You're going to be here for three days.
Hotel:	You don't know. Does Student A know a good hotel?

SECTION 18 *(page 70)*

Scoring

1-3	People may think you're rude and officious. You need to study this unit on social interaction very carefully.
4-7	Sometimes you aren't very polite. Maybe you're embarrassed in social situations. Don't be afraid to speak to people.
8-12	You try to be polite and helpful, but sometimes you don't want to get involved - you don't pay enough attention to other people's problems.
13-16	You're polite and often charming. But be careful! Perhaps sometimes you aren't assertive enough.

SECTION 19 *(page 115)*
Student B

You work for a mail order company, Gifts by Post. Student A is going to call you with a complaint. Ask the name and address. You will then find the information on your computer terminal. During the conversation, try to use this sentence: *This has never happened before.*

GIFTS BY POST

▲▼ index by name index by address index by post code

File name: SMITH, J
Mailing address:
23 STIRLING STREET
LEEDS
Post code: LS7 6TY

CREDIT CARD:
type: MASTERVISA
number: 0000-7788-0022-6633
expiry: 08/10

CURRENT ORDER:
Sent: May 20

003-567	Hand Towels	blue	2
004-112	T-shirt	medium	1
096-225	Phone book covers	–	2

SECTION 20 *(page 51)*
Student A

You are going to work in pairs. You have all of photo 1, but only a part of photo 2. Student B has all of photo 2, but only part of photo 1. You are going to ask each other questions to find out as much information as possible. Student B will begin by asking you about photo 1. Then you will ask about photo 2.

This is the complete photo 1.

This is a section of photo 2.

SECTION 21 *(page 130)*
Student C

Some ideas for *compromise:*

- At present there are five tea ladies and one vending machine. The company could rent two or three more vending machines without sacking tea ladies.
- When tea ladies retire, they need not be replaced. However, no one would be sacked.
- Voluntary redundancy – the company could ask if any tea ladies wanted to leave or to retire early. It could then pay them (e.g.) a year's wages for voluntary redundancy.
- Each department could choose whether they wanted tea ladies or vending machines.
- The company could do another survey. This would not be done by Daniel Elgin because his survey was biased.
- The company could ask employees to pay more for the tea ladies' service, therefore reducing the cost to the company.

SECTION 22 *(page 11)*
Student B

Work in pairs.

Role-play 1: Taking the order

Student A is going to order a meal. Write down their order. Then deliver the meal to them.

Role-play 2: Ordering a meal

You are in a restaurant with your friends, Michael and Sarah. Order a meal from Student A. Student A is going to write down your order. On the menu there are notes. M = Michael, S = Sarah, Y = you.

TOURIST MENU

First course
Mushroom soup S
Chicken soup M
Tomato juice Y

Main Course
Fish & chips Y
Omelette S
Macaroni Cheese M

Sweets
Strawberry ice-cream S
Apple pie Y
Fruit salad M

SECTION 23 *(page 36)*
Student A

This is your reading text. Think about where you are going to pause. Then try reading to the rest of the class. Try to make eye contact with as many people as you can while you're reading.

> Professor Morrison is a famous scientist. She teaches at the University of Oxford. Her lectures aren't popular. She always reads from her notes, and she never looks at the students in her class. She never makes eye contact. They see only the top of her head when she is giving a lecture.

SECTION 24 *(page 107)*

Who would you tip?

In the USA you would tip all of these people. In a very formal restaurant, you might even tip the busboy (assistant waiter) and wine waiter as well. In Britain, tipping is less frequent but it would be normal to give tips, except to the head waiter. If a hairdresser is the owner of a salon, it is not necessary to leave a tip.

How much would you tip?

BRITAIN   10% is the general rule, but in more expensive restaurants tip 12.5% to 15%. You don't have to tip if the menu says *service included*. Don't tip if service is bad. Calculate your tip on the price before the restaurant adds Value Added Tax (VAT). Tip hotel porters about 50p per bag.

USA   Tips are a major part of people's income in service industries. Waiters are paid very little, but expect large gratuities. 10% to 15% is fine. However, large hotels are beginning to suggest the amount of a tip. In Orlando some hotels 'suggest' 18-20%. In New York restaurants 15% is a minimum. Tip more for excellent service. You needn't tip if there is a service charge for (e.g.) room service. Calculate your tip on the price before taxes are added. Tip bellhops $1 per bag, car valets $1 to $2, hotel doormen $1 if they find you a taxi.

SPAIN   In most restaurants a few coins is enough. In taxis, don't wait for small change.

JAPAN   Don't tip. People don't give or expect gratuities. (Visitors from Europe and the USA think this is wonderful.)

How would you show appreciation after a lecture?

What kind of lecture was it? Usually polite clapping is correct.

What would you take to dinner at a business acquaintance's home?

A gift is not essential, but something inexpensive from your country would be appreciated. As some people are on a diet, flowers are the best choice if you don't have anything else. Bottles of wine are usually for more informal parties with younger people (unless the wine is a gift from your country). An expensive gift would be embarrassing.

How would you thank a foreign business acquaintance?

It depends. It's often a good idea to write a short 'thank you' note after you've returned home. Any cash gift would be a bribe, and very embarrassing.

SECTION 25 *(page 74)*

Women talk more about feelings and relationships.
Men talk more about things.
Men use fewer adjectives than women, and describe things in less detail.
Men ask fewer questions in conversation.
Men rarely discuss their personal life.
Women use more polite formulas than men.
Men tell more jokes.
Men interrupt more than women (three times more often).
Women more often smile when listening. Men more often frown.
Women are more attentive listeners (smiling, nodding, agreeing).
Women use a greater range of intonation than men.
Men ask others for help less often than women.
Men get to the point of the conversation more quickly than women do.
Men make more direct statements. They begin sentences with *It is …, We will …*
Women make more indirect statements. They begin sentences with *I think …, I hope …, I feel …*
Men use more quantifiers (words like *all, none, every, always*).
Women use more qualifiers (words like *a bit, kind of*).

SECTION 26 *(page 130)*
Student B

Some arguments *against* vending machines:

- Tea breaks are a social occasion. Everyone stops at the same time. This is an opportunity for people to talk to each other.
- The conversation during tea breaks is often about work. As a result problems are discussed informally.
- If you didn't have tea breaks, you'd probably need formal meetings to discuss company problems.
- The tea ladies collect empty cups and take them away.
- Nobody would collect the empty disposable cups so offices would become untidy. As a result, the company would need more cleaners.
- If the tea ladies were sacked, employees would be upset. They'd feel that the company had no sympathy for people and no loyalty towards its staff.
- They'd feel 'tea ladies today; me tomorrow'.
- Because people have to walk to vending machines, drinks are often spilled on the floors.
- Some people are technophobic – they have problems with machines.

See also Sharon's argument (page 128) on the disadvantages of vending machines.

SECTION 27 *(page 84)*
Student B

You have to interrupt Student A, who is your supervisor. When you are correcting a fact, don't forget to put *emphasis* on the information which is wrong, and on your correction. You feel the accusation is unfair for these reasons:

- Actually the time is 9.46.
- So you're 45 minutes late, not an hour.
- You were late last week, but this is only the second time this month.
- Actually, two or three of your co-workers are sometimes late.
- You leave your home in plenty of time too. Your train broke down.
- Mrs Macintosh never gets to the office before 9.30.
- You couldn't telephone. The train was in a tunnel.

SECTION 28 *(page 31)*
Student B

Ask Student A questions and try to find information about the three pictures on the left. This is information about the three pictures on the right. Student A will ask you about them.

Picture 4
Leonard Cohen is a Canadian rock singer and poet. He became famous in the 1960s. He was born in 1934.

Picture 5
Kate Adie is a British TV journalist. She is well known for her reports from war zones for the BBC. She was born in 1945.

Picture 6
Gianni De Michelis is an Italian politician. He was Foreign Minister in the Italian government. He was born in 1940.

SECTION 29 *(page 81)*
Student B

Role-play 1: You have the bad news. Let your partner speak first.

You are the the sales director of Acme Vacuum Cleaners. Student A is a sales representative for your company. You have some bad news for Student A. The company has not done well this year, and as a result the managing director has decided to lose 50% of the sales representatives. The most recently appointed representatives are the first to go. Unfortunately, Student A is one of them.

Role-play 2: You have the good news. Speak first.

You own a valuable old car. It's 35 years old, but it goes well and you still use it at weekends. The problem is that you need money. You don't want to sell the car, but you have to. After all, it stays in the garage most of the time. This afternoon, someone offered you a lot of money for the car (more than it is worth). Your financial problems are over! You are very happy. You are going to tell a member of your family the good news.

SECTION 30 *(page 69)*
Student B

You are going to role-play a conversation with Student A. You are one of the people in the cartoon. You are guests at the Hotel Splendide. It's your first day. You are going to stay for two weeks in the best room in the hotel. You haven't seen the notice (Pool rules & regulations). A hotel employee comes over and speaks to you.

- Ask what the employee wants.
- Reply that you are a guest, and that you're staying for two weeks.
- Explain that it is your first day and that you haven't seen a notice.
- Say that you have nearly finished your ice-cream. You have been very careful, and nothing has fallen into the pool.
- Repeat that you have nearly finished. You are trying to have a nice time and enjoy yourselves. Say that you are a guest, and that you have paid a lot of money for your room.
- Refuse to get out of the pool. Ask to see the manager of the hotel immediately.
- Continue the conversation!

Change roles. Improvise another conversation about some different rules of the pool.

SECTION 31 *(page 36)*
Student B

This is your reading text. Think about where you are going to pause. Then try reading to the rest of the class. Try to make eye contact with as many people as you can while you're reading.

> Postal workers often have problems with dogs. Dogs sometimes attack them when they are delivering letters. One postal worker gives this advice. 'Don't be afraid of dogs. Always look them straight in the eye, and don't move. After a few seconds the dog will move away.'

SECTION 32 *(page 51)*
Student B

You are going to work in pairs. You have only part of photo 1, but all of photo 2. Student B has all of photo 1, but only part of photo 2. You are going to ask each other questions to find out as much information as possible. You begin by asking Student A about photo 1. Then Student A will ask you about photo 2.

This is a section of photo 1.

This is the complete photo 2.

SECTION 33 *(page 69)*
Student A

You are going to role-play a conversation with Student B. You are a new assistant manager at the Hotel Splendide. You are on your way to a meeting. You see Student B and a friend in the pool. You can see them in the cartoon. What are you going to do? They are breaking the rules of the swimming pool. You go over and speak to them.

- Introduce yourself.
- Ask them if they are guests of the hotel.
- Ask them if they have seen the notice (Pool rules & regulations).
- Tell them that food and drink is not permitted in the pool area.
- Offer to take the food and drink to a poolside table.
- Ask them to get out of the pool.
- Continue the conversation!

Change roles. Improvise another conversation about some different rules of the pool.

SECTION 34 *(page 31)*
Student A

This is information about the three pictures on the left. Student B will ask you about them. Ask Student B questions and try to find information about the three pictures on the right.

Picture 1
Dr Rob Buckman is British and he's a medical doctor. He is also a TV presenter and writer. He was born in 1948.

Picture 2
Mae Jemison is American. She is a doctor and a scientist and was an astronaut in 1992. She was born in 1956.

Picture 3
Richard Branson is a business tycoon. He was the owner of Virgin Records, then chief of Virgin Atlantic Airways. He's a famous balloonist, too. He was born in 1950.

SECTION 35 *(page 53)*
Student A

You are going to do two role-plays.

Role-play 1: Interviewer
You are the interviewer. Ask questions about the applicant's résumé, plus these extra questions.

Did you have a good journey here today?
Did you find my office easily?
Have you been to (this town) before?
Which subjects did you enjoy most at school?
What do you do during your free time?
What sort of things are you good at?
What sort of job would you like in ten years time?

Role-play 2: Applicant
You are the applicant. Answer the interviewer's questions, and ask these questions about the job.

What is the salary?
How many days holiday are there a year?
Can I work overtime?
Can I get promotion in this job?

SECTION 36 *(page 84)*
Student A

You have to interrupt Student B, who is the museum guide. Student B is making a number of factual mistakes which you want to correct. When you are correcting a fact, don't forget to put *emphasis* on the information which is wrong, and on your correction.

- Leonardo was Italian, not Spanish.
- Leonardo lived in Florence, not in Venice.
- Leonardo was dead in 1603. He was born in 1452, and he died in 1519.
- Leonardo was working in the late fifteenth and early sixteenth centuries.
- The Louvre Museum is in Paris, not Rome.
- The first owner was the King of France. (It's true that he kept the painting in his bathroom, though!)

SECTION 37 *(page 98)*
Student C

This is your basic story. Try to add details. The words in (brackets) should help you.

Someone (*who?*) was taking an elephant along a street (*why? was there a circus? was it going to a zoo?*). They stopped near some cars (*where?*). Suddenly the elephant walked over and sat on a small car (*what make? what colour?*). It seems the elephant had a seat of the same colour that it used in a show (*where?*). The car was damaged. Later (*when?*) the car's owner (*who?*) was driving along when the police stopped them to ask about the damage. The owner told the story to the police who didn't believe them (*so, what did the police do?*).

SECTION 38 *(page 115)*
Student A

You have ordered some items from a mail order company. This is a copy of your order form. This morning a parcel arrived from the company. The towels were blue, the T-shirt was XL (extra large), the leather phone book covers were black, and the Scotland calendar wasn't there at all. Call the company to complain. During the conversation, try to use this sentence: *This has caused me a lot of inconvenience!*

Gifts by Post **ORDER FORM**

Send to: Gifts by Post, PO BOX 32, Poole, Dorset, BH13 4TT
Telephone orders: 01202 -188765 Fax: 01202-1654933

item	colour	code	size	quantity	price	total
Hand towel	pink	003-567	—	2	£5.00	£10.00
'Scotland' calendar	—	098-771	—	1	£7.95	£7.95
'Smiling Faces' T-shirts	white	004-112	medium	1	£16.25	£16.25
Leather phone book covers	brown	096-225	—	2	£11.95	£23.90
				Plus Postage & Packing		£2.50
				TOTAL		£60.60

METHOD OF PAYMENT

☐ I enclose cheque / PO payable to **Gifts by Post**
☑ Please charge my credit / debit card for the items I have ordered: ☑ VISA ☐ ACCESS ☐ AMEX

Card no: .....0000 - 7788 - 0022 - 6633................. Expiry date: ...08/10......................

Cardholder's signature ....J.Smith..

Name: ....J. Smith..

Address: ....23 Stirling Street , Leeds, LS7 6TY..

Active Grammar appendix

TO THE STUDENT

This is not a grammar book. This section explains some important basic points of grammar, with short simple exercises on some of the points. You should look at a grammar book for extra information. You can find more exercises in the Language Focus sections of this book and in the Workbook.

ABILITY

● *can, can't, could, couldn't* are used to express ability:
> **Can** you drive?
> Help! I **can't** swim!
> **Could** you understand what he was saying?
> She **couldn't** dance very well.

can has a present and a future meaning:
> I **can** finish it tomorrow.

could has a past meaning:
> I **could** swim when I was five.

● We can also use *be able to* for ability, and it's easier to do this in the past and future:
> I can't do it now. I'll **be able to** do it later.
> They **were able to** complete the job last week.

We use *be able to* in the present perfect tense:
> I've **been able to** type three of the letters, but I **haven't been able to** type the other one.

The difference is very small, and often doesn't matter. We are more likely to use *be able to* when something was difficult:
> At first we **couldn't** do it because there was a problem, but finally we **were able to** do it.

ADJECTIVES

Adjectives don't change for number or person:
> a **big** book   **big** books
> He's **angry**   She's **angry**   They're **angry**

Adjectives usually come before nouns:
> He's got a **new watch**. NOT He's got a ~~watch new~~.

Match the adjectives in Column A with their opposites in Column B.

Column A	Column B
happy	relaxed
co-operative	interested
bored	warm
cold	unhappy
nervous	unco-operative

● Many adjectives, like past participles, end in *-ed*:
> *open-necked shirt, polished shoes, tailored clothes, a suntanned face, grilled fish, coloured paper*

Complete the spaces.

1 A man with long hair is a *long-haired man*.
2 A carpet that someone fits into a room is a ..... .
3 An egg that someone has boiled is a ..... .
4 A programme that someone has recorded is a ..... .
5 A woman with blue eyes is a ..... .
6 A car that someone designed well is a ..... .

ADVERBS OF MOVEMENT

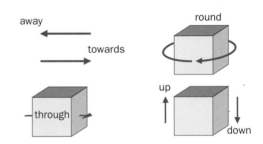

See also **prepositions of place** below.

ADVERBS OF MANNER

● Adverbs of manner tell us how something is done:
> He speaks **clearly**.
> She works **quickly** and **efficiently**.
> They did it very **well**.

Most adverbs of manner are formed by adding *-ly* to the adjective:

Adjective	Adverb
clear	clearly
bad	badly
nice	nicely

There are important irregular examples:

Adjective	Adverb
good	well
fast	fast
hard	hard

● Some adverbs are losing their *-ly* ending in everyday speech. Examples are *slowly / slow, quickly / quick* and in American English *really / real*. In American English, you will hear:
> It was **really** difficult / It was **real** difficult.

Complete the spaces with adverbs.

1   She's a good singer. She sings ..... .
2   They work ..... . They're hard workers.
3   He's a bad driver. He drives ..... .
4   I walk ..... . I'm a fast walker.
5   They're a loud band. They play ..... .

ADVICE

● Ways of giving advice:
*You **should** drive more carefully.*
*You **shouldn't** drive so fast.*
*You **ought to** drive more carefully.*
*You **ought not to** drive so fast.*

should is used more for personal advice. *ought to* is sometimes less personal. We talk about authority with *ought to*:
*They **ought to** do something about road accidents.*
(Who? The police? The government? Drivers? We're not really sure).

● We can use these other ways of giving advice:
Why don't you *(see your doctor)?*
If I were you, I'd *(see my doctor).*
You'd better *(see your doctor).*

Often when giving advice, we begin with phrases like *I think … / In my opinion …* :
I think *you should see a doctor.*
In my opinion, *you should see a doctor.*

ALLOWED TO, PERMITTED TO

These usually appear in the **passive** form:
*Smoking **is not allowed** / **permitted** on aeroplanes.*
*People **are not allowed to** / **permitted to** smoke on aeroplanes.*

Active forms are possible with *allow / permit*:
*They don't **allow** / **permit** you to smoke at school.*
*They don't **allow** / **permit** smoking in the airport lounge.*

See also **supposed to** below.

ARTICLES

Indefinite articles: *a / an*
Definite article: *the*

● Use *a* before the sound of a consonant:
a *pen,* ***a*** *bus,* ***a*** *tree,* ***a*** *tall woman,* ***a*** *nice apple*

Use *an* before the sound of a vowel:
an *apple,* ***an*** *egg,* ***an*** *ice-cream,* ***an*** *orange,* ***an*** *umbrella,* ***an*** *old man,* ***an*** *empty box*

Remember that the important thing is sound, not spelling. So we say: ***a*** *uniform,* ***a*** *union,* ***a*** *European* because the sound is /j/.

We say: ***an*** *honest person,* ***an*** *hour* because the 'h' is silent.

● We use *the* when we expect someone to know which thing we are talking about:
*Could you pass me **the** butter?*
*I'm going to **the** dentist tomorrow.*

We do not generally use *the* with uncountable and plural nouns:
Petrol is expensive. / I like biscuits.
NOT ~~The petrol is expensive. / I like the biscuits.~~

We use *the* when there is only one example of the thing we are talking about:
the *sun,* ***the*** *Earth,* ***the*** *British,* ***the*** *airport*
(There are many airports, but only one is important to us now.)

We use *the* for many words connected to weather and geography:
the *snow,* ***the*** *wind,* ***the*** *mountains,* ***The*** *River Nile,* ***The*** *Pacific Ocean*

● Note the pronunciation:
/ðiː/ before a vowel sound
/ðə/ before a consonant sound

Say these phrases aloud.

1   the apple   6   the artist
2   the news   7   the ice-cream
3   the United States   8   the hour
4   the EU   9   The BBC
5   the 1.30 flight   10   the PIN number

Put *a / an / the* in these sentences.

1   The police officer is wearing ...... uniform.
2   I'd like ...... apple, please.
3   Where's ...... manager of the company?
4   ...... Prince of Wales was here yesterday.
5   It's ...... enormous building.
6   That's ...... biggest building in the world.
7   There's ...... hour before we have lunch.
8   Do you know ...... right answer to this question?

COMPARISON OF ADJECTIVES

● We compare short adjectives by adding *-er* and *-est*:

adjective	comparative	superlative
quiet	quieter	quietest
new	newer	newest
big	bigger	biggest
early	earlier	earliest
large	larger	largest

We compare longer adjectives by putting *more, less, most* or *least* in front of them:

adjective	comparative	superlative
important	more important	the most important
	less important	the least important

Some common adjectives are irregular:

adjective	comparative	superlative
good	better	the best
bad	worse	the worst
far	further	the furthest

● In traditional grammar the comparative is used to compare two things:
> This one's good, but that one's **better**.

The superlative is used for three or more things:
> Those ones are good, but this one's **the best**.

In modern speech, the superlative is often used for comparing just two things:
> This one's good, but that one's **the best**.

● Look at these examples.

than is important with comparatives:
> This chair's more comfortable **than** that one.
> My new computer's faster and more powerful **than** my old one. It's less expensive too.

the is important with superlatives:
> That office is **the** largest.
> She's the most important person in **the** company.
> It's **the** least expensive car.

Write a list of six things that you and your partner have. Compare them.
> *My pen is less expensive than her pen, but it's newer.*

Work with another pair. Compare the things on your list.
> *Maria's house is the furthest from the school.*

Adverbs ending in *-ly* are compared by adding *more, most, less* and *least*:
> She ran **more quickly** then he did.
> He works **less carefully** than I do.
> Everyone in the car was injured, but the driver was injured **the least seriously**.
> The London factory worked **the most efficiently**.

● With many adverbs, the comparative of the adverb is the same as the comparative of the adjective:
> They came **later** than us.
> We arrived **earlier** than them.
> The car went **better** with unleaded fuel.

● Some adverbs are in a state of change. You will see both *more slowly* and *slower, more quickly* and *quicker*.

CONDITIONALS – TYPE 1

● Conditional sentences are sentences with *if* and *unless*.

The basic form of type 1 conditionals is:
> **if + a present tense + comma + future**

> **If it rains, I'll take** an umbrella.
> **If you're** busy, **I'll call** later.
> **If we've missed** the bus, **we'll take** a taxi.

or
> **future + if + a present tense**

> **I'll take** an umbrella **if it rains**.
> **I'll call** later **if you're** busy.
> **We'll take** a taxi **if we've missed** the bus.

● Modals can have a future meaning:
> I **can** call later if you're busy.
> If it's raining we **must** take an umbrella.

In all these sentences we are talking about something that is a real possibility.

Put the verbs in brackets in the correct form.

1 If I (be) late, I (phone) from the station.
2 If you (be) in London, we (meet) for lunch.
3 They (not like) it if we (not make) an appointment.
4 She (rent) a car if she (go) to Los Angeles.
5 If you (need) more photocopies, I (do) them for you.

CONDITIONALS – TYPE 2

● We use type 2 conditionals when we are imagining something.

The basic form is:

if + **a past tense** + **comma** + *would / could / should / might*

If I won a lot of money, I'd go to Hawaii.
If I knew the answer, I would tell you.
If she didn't go to work, her boss would be angry.
If we weren't at school, we could go to the beach.

or

would / could / should / might + **if** + **a past tense**

I'd go to Tahiti if I won a lot of money.
I would tell you if I knew the answer.
Her boss would be angry if she didn't go to work.

● *If I were you …*
were replaces *was* in type 2 conditionals:
If I were you … If she were here … If it were mine …

However, while people usually remember to say *If I were you …*, you will often hear *was* with *he, she, it*:
If she was here.
If it was mine.

What would you do if these things happened?

1 You win a lottery.
   If I won a lottery, I'd buy a new house.
2 You can go anywhere in the world.
3 You meet your boss at a disco.
4 You see a robbery.
5 You find a lot of money in the street.

CONDITIONALS – TYPE 3

We use type 3 conditionals when we are imagining something about the past.

The basic form is:

if + **a past perfect tense** + **comma** + *would / could / should / might* + **have** + **past participle**

If I had been there, I would have enjoyed myself.
If it hadn't rained, we wouldn't've got wet.
If only I'd known, I'd've called you earlier.

You can reverse the order:
I would have enjoyed myself if I had been there.

Choose the correct word.

1 If I had (lose / lost) my keys, I couldn't (have / had) opened the door.
2 If only I (had /would) known, I wouldn't have (call / called) you.
3 I (will / would) have helped if I'd (been / were) there.

CONTRAST (*HOWEVER* ETC.)

It was difficult. We did it.

The ideas in these two sentences contrast. We express contrast in several ways.

● *however* introduces a new sentence:
*It was difficult. **However**, we did it.*

● *although* introduces a verb phrase. The two sentences are connected with a comma:
***Although** it was difficult, we did it.*
Note that *although* goes with the problem, not the solution.

● *In spite of* introduces a noun or noun phrase:
***In spite of** the difficulties, we did it.*

COULD, COULDN'T

could has three uses:

– as the past tense of can:
*I **could** swim when I was five.*
– as the conditional form of can:
*If I **could** ski, I'd go to Austria for a holiday.*
– for polite requests – because conditional forms are more polite:
***Could** I have a drink, please?*

COUNTABLE / UNCOUNTABLE NOUNS

In English there is an important difference between countable nouns and uncountable nouns. Uncountable nouns always take a singular verb.

Countable (units; things)	Uncountable (mass; stuff)
There's a book.	There's some water.
Is there a book?	Is there any water?
Are there any books?	
There aren't any books.	There isn't any water.
There are a lot.	There is a lot.
There are a few.	There is a little.
There aren't enough.	There is enough.
How many are there?	How much is there?

Some words are difficult. For example, *peas* are countable. *Rice* is uncountable. Remember that *water* is uncountable, but *bottles of water, litres of water, glasses of water* are all countable.

Write *C* or *U* next to these words.

milk	bread	mushrooms
tomatoes	tomato juice	pasta
rolls	petrol	time
hours	cans of pasta	money
dollars	newspapers	paper
spaghetti	beans	litres of milk

DEDUCTION AND SPECULATION

● We make deductions about the present and the future with *can / must / may / might* + **be**:
*He **must be** there by now.*

We make deductions about the past with *can / must / can't* + **have** + **past participle**:
*She **must have done** it.*

I	must	have	done it.
You	can't		been there.
He	could		seen it.
She	may		found them.
We	might		
They			

● When we are speculating we don't know the facts. We speculate about the present with *may, might* and *could*:
*I **might** be late.*
*It **could** be mine. I'm not sure.*

We speculate about the past with *may have (done)/ might have (done) / could have (done)*:
*I haven't got my diary. I **may have left** it at home.*

fact	It is true.
	It was true.
	It happened.
	It will happen.
deduction (present and past)	It must be true.
	It can't be true.
	It must have been true.
	It can't have been true.
	It must have happened.
	It can't have happened.
speculation (past, present and future)	It may / might / could be true.
	It may / might / could happen.
	It may / might / could have been true.
	It may / might / could have happened.

Make sentences with *must be / can't be / might be*.

1 It's not a plane – that's impossible!
2 I don't know really. I think perhaps it's mine …
3 She's got a big car, she lives in Hollywood and everyone knows who she is.

Make sentences with *may / must / can't have (done)*.

1 A colleague hasn't arrived for work today.
2 You can't find your purse or wallet. You've looked everywhere in this room.
3 A friend has just said, 'I've got two million pounds!'

DETERMINERS

Determiners include other grammatical areas:

● articles:
the / a / an

● demonstrative pronouns:

	near	far
singular	this	that
plural	these	those

● possessive adjectives:
my / your / his / her / their / our / its

● quantifiers:
some / no / any / every / each / either / much / a few / both / one / three

DURING

during is a time word. It introduces a noun or noun phrase:
*He ate an ice-cream **during** the film.*
*She got angry **during** the meeting with the Sales Manager.*

If a verb phrase follows the time word, use *while*, not *during*:
*He ate an ice-cream **while** he was watching TV.*

EACH OTHER / ONE ANOTHER

I know her. She knows me.
We know each other.

In traditional grammar, *each other* is used for two people, *one another* for three or more people:
*I have a group of friends. We've known **one another** since we were children.*

However, in everyday conversation *each other* often replaces *one another*:

> I have a group of friends. We've known **each other** since we were children.

Compare with **reflexive pronouns** below.

Rewrite these sentences using *each other / one another* or a reflexive pronoun.

1 He hit me. I hit him. *We hit each other.*
2 He hurt himself. I hurt myself. *We hurt ourselves.*
3 He likes her and she likes him.
4 I work by myself and you work by yourself.
5 He's pleased with himself and she's pleased with herself.
6 We know them and they know us.
7 She met me and I met her.

EXPRESSING OPINIONS

Opinion words and phrases can come before sentences giving your opinion, e.g. when talking about jobs in the future:

I'm sure I'm certain I think I reckon I guess I hope	there'll be	more fewer etc.	teachers lawyers	because because of...

FIGURES

Note the use of commas and full stops:

write	say
1.5 / 1·5	one point five
100	one hundred / a hundred
105	one hundred and five / one oh five
1,500	one thousand five hundred
1,000,000	one million
30%	thirty per cent
30°	thirty degrees (Celsius)
3 + 2	three plus two
3 - 2	three minus two
3 x 2	three times two
6 ÷ 2	six divided by two

FOR AND SINCE

for and *since* are usually used with perfect tenses: the present perfect, the past perfect, the present perfect continuous, the past perfect continuous.

- *for* is used for periods of time:
  *I've been here **for** (two hours / days / weeks / months / years / a long time / ages).*
  *I've been waiting **for** (ten minutes).*
  I'd had a headache for two days.
  *I'd been studying **for** a year when I took the exam.*

- *since* is used for points in time:
  *I've known them **since** (Tuesday / January / the summer / 1995).*
  *I've been living here **since** (April).*
  *I'd had a headache **since** the accident.*
  *I'd been living there **since** the previous year.*

Complete the spaces with *for* or *since*.

1 I'd been worried about her ...... a long time.
2 I've been very busy ...... ten o'clock.
3 She's had the job ...... February 3rd.
4 The band have been playing together ...... last Spring.
5 I'd been driving ...... three hours before I saw a petrol station.

FORMS OF ADDRESS

- General

Mr / Mrs / Miss / Ms

Only use these with a family name, e.g. *Ms Perkins, Mr Alderton*.
Never use with a first name. ~~Mrs Jane.~~

You can also use *Master* for young boys, but nowadays it's frequent only on airline tickets (*Mstr*).
Note punctuation:　UK:　Mr / Mrs / Ms
　　　　　　　　　　USA:　Mr. / Mrs. / Ms.

Sir / Madam / Ma'am / Miss

These are used instead of a name, e.g. *Yes, Ma'am*. This is more common in the USA than in Britain. *Miss* can also be used instead of a name, and is a common form of address for schoolteachers.

- Jobs

The list shows some jobs which are used both instead of and with a name, e.g. *Excuse me, Nurse!* or *Excuse me, Nurse Williams!*

Some are marked *. You can use these instead of a name, e.g. *Excuse me, Chef.* You can't use these with a name.

Academic	*Dr / Doctor / Prof. / Professor* UK: Teachers are not addressed as 'professor'. A professor is a senior university teacher.
Medical	*Doctor / Nurse / Sister / Chargenurse*
Military	*Sergeant / Captain / Colonel*
Police	*Officer */ Constable* (UK) / *Sergeant / Inspector / Superintendent* (UK) / *Lieutenant, Captain , Chief* (USA)
Political	*Minister*, Prime Minister,** (UK) *Senator, Governor, Mayor,* (Mr) *President* (USA)
Religious	*Reverend* (Protestant) / *Father* (Catholic)
Other jobs	*Waiter * Chef * Driver**

Note that most jobs do not have a form of address.

Which of these sentences is incorrect? Put a cross (✗) next to them.

1 Can I have my medicine, Sister?
2 Where's Dr Sabatini?
3 I want to see Mrs Anna.
4 Is Chef Martinu in the kitchen?
5 Do you know Architect Suzuki?
6 I'm very, very sorry, Sergeant.
7 Hi, teacher!
8 Please answer the question, Senator.

FREQUENCY ADVERBS

● Meaning:
always – 100% of the time
usually, generally, normally – most of the time
often, frequently – many times
sometimes – 1-99% of the time
occasionally – only a few times
seldom, rarely, hardly ever – very few times, 0.1% of the time
never – 0% of the time

● Frequency adverbs come before the main verb in the present simple tense and present perfect tense:
*They don't **often** watch TV.*
*She **usually** has sugar in her coffee.*
*I've **always** liked rock music.*
*He's **never** been to Ireland.*

● Frequency adverbs come after the verb *to be*:
*I'm **hardly ever** late for work.*
*We were **often** tired.*

Put appropriate frequency adverbs into the correct places in the sentences below.

1 The sun rises in the east.
2 I've been to Antarctica.
3 It rains in England.
4 It rains in the Sahara Desert.
5 It is cold in Canada in winter.
6 TV programmes are violent.
7 I am late for work.
8 I drink tea.

FUTURE CONTINUOUS

● The basic structure is:

will / shall + be + present participle
I'll be working upstairs when you arrive.
*Just think about it! This time next week we'll be lying on a beach. We **won't be working**!*

● The future continuous is also used to talk about present time when we're speculating about what might be happening a long distance away:

*Los Angeles is three hours behind New York. It's 11 a.m. here in New York. My brother **will be having** breakfast in Los Angeles about now.*

Note that *is having* is also possible.

Think about people you know who are a long distance away. What will they be doing now? Ask and answer with a partner.

FUTURE SIMPLE

Affirmative and negative

I We	'll will won't shall (formal British) shan't (very formal Br.)	be there at 5.30. do it tomorrow.
You They He She It	'll will won't	

● *will* and *shall also* have several non-future uses. Traditional British grammars use *shall* for the first person, but people usually use the contraction *'ll*, and *won't* is the normal negative even for those speakers who use *shall*. Use *shall* in suggestions and offers, but don't use it for the future simple:
***Shall** I do it for you?*
***Shall** we go to the beach?*

Work with a partner. Make a timetable for tomorrow. Ask and answer.

Where will you be at 2 o'clock?
Who will you have lunch with?
What will you have for lunch? etc.

GOING TO FUTURE

to be + ***going to (do)*** is used to talk about the future:
*What are you **going to do** this evening?*
*I'm **going to** stay at home.*
*He's **going to** play football for his country one day!*

You can say *going to go*, but more often people just say *going*:
*We aren't **going to go** on holiday this year.*
*We aren't **going** on holiday this year.*

See also **present continuous** below.

GREETING FORMULAS

Informal			Formal
Hi	Hello	Good morning	How do you do (first meeting)
How are you doing* (USA)	How are you*	Good afternoon	
How's things*		Good evening	
How's it going*	Good day (Australia)		

● The response to most greetings is simply to repeat the greeting. The greetings with an asterisk (*) need an answer. e.g. *Very well, thanks.*

The response to *How do you do* is *How do you do* in British English, but in American English, people often answer the 'question' (e.g. *I'm very well*). You may see *How do you do* with or without a question mark. In the USA it more often has a question mark.

Goodnight is only used for saying *Goodbye,* never for saying *Hello.*

What are the greetings that produce these responses?

1 OK.
2 Not bad.
3 Good afternoon.
4 I'm very well, thanks.
5 Fine, thank you. And you?
6 Hi.
7 All right.

IMPERATIVES

We use imperatives to give commands and instructions:

affirmative	negative
Be careful.	Don't be silly.
Be on time.	Don't be late.
Do this.	Don't do that.
Turn it on.	Don't turn it off.
Come here.	Don't go there.
Turn right.	Don't turn left.

Give a partner five instructions. Your partner should follow them.

INDIRECT QUESTIONS

● Direct questions are used:
– when you expect someone to know the answer.
Where is it?
– in informal situations, e.g. with friends.

● Indirect questions are used:
– when you aren't sure whether they know the answer or not:
Do you know where it is?
– to be more polite:
Do you know where it is?
Can you tell me where it is?
– in more formal situations.
– when asking an embarrassing question.

● *Yes / No* questions form indirect questions with *if* and *whether*:

Direct question	Indirect question
Is it new?	Do you know if it's new? Do you know whether it's new?
Can she swim?	Do you know if she can swim? Do you know whether she can swim?
Did it go?	Do you know if it went? Do you know whether it went?

Yes / No questions with *do / does / did:*
Did she go?
Do you know if she went?
Does he understand?
Do you know if he understands?

● *Wh-* questions form indirect questions like this:

Direct question	Indirect question
What is it?	Do you know what it is?
Who are they?	Do you know who they are?

Wh- questions with *do / does / did:*
>   *Where did he go?*
>   *Do you know where he went?*

Look at the word order in these direct and indirect questions.

Yes / No questions

Direct form	Indirect form
Is <u>it</u> far?	Do you know if <u>it</u> **is** far?

Wh–questions

Direct form	Indirect form
Where **is** <u>it</u>?	Do you know where <u>it</u> **is**?

Questions with *do / does / did*

Direct form	Indirect form
Did <u>she</u> go?	**Do** you know if <u>she</u> **went**?
Where **does** <u>he</u> live?	**Do** you know where <u>he</u> **lives**?

Form indirect questions from these direct questions.

1   Are they coming to the party?
2   Does he like English food?
3   Can she play the guitar?
4   When does it begin?
5   Who will be there?
6   When is it going to finish?

INFINITIVES

● Infinitives are the basic form, or name of a verb:
>   *to do, to eat, to live*

Some books call both *to eat* and *eat* infinitives. In this book we have called the form without *to* the **bare** infinitive.

There are other types of infinitive as well:

infinitive	to eat
continuous infinitive	to be eating
perfect infinitive	to have eaten
passive infinitive	to be eaten

Infinitives do not usually show time or tense, unlike other forms (*eating, eats, ate, eaten*).

They have many uses:
–   after verbs:
>   *I want **to do** it. I tried **to phone** you.*
–   after adjectives:
>   *It's nice **to see** you. I was sorry **to hear** your news.*
–   after nouns:
>   *I need a good book **to read**. Have you got a pen to **lend me**?*
–   to express purpose:
>   *I'm going to London **to buy** some clothes.*
–   with *it's time... :*
>   *It's time **to go**.*

● Verbs that are usually followed by infinitives include:
>   *agree, ask, choose, expect, hope, learn, manage, offer, prefer, promise, refuse, seem, try, want*

See also *-ing* **form or infinitive?** below.

-ING FORM OR INFINITIVE?

● The present participle form (*swimming, working*) can be used as a verb. It is called an *-ing* form when it is used as a noun, adjective or adverb. When used as a noun, it is also called a **gerund** or verbal noun:
>   *You've been **working** very hard.* (verb)
>   ***Working** mothers need better nursery schools.* (adjective)
>   ***Swimming** is good exercise.* (noun)
>   *He left the room **crying**.* (adverb)

● Some verbs are usually followed by an infinitive form, others are usually followed by an *-ing* form. Verbs usually followed by an *-ing* form include:
>   *like, enjoy, love, hate, start, finish, begin, avoid, suggest, think about, can't help, can't stand (i.e. hate), mind, practise, understand*
>   *You should practise **playing** the piano every day.*
>   *Do you mind **helping**?*

● Some of these verbs are followed by an object before the *-ing* form:
>   *I don't like people **giving** me orders.*
>   *You can't stop him **talking**!*

● Some verbs can be followed by either an *-ing* form or an infinitive. Sometimes there is a change of meaning:
>   *I stopped **watching** TV. I stopped to answer the phone.*
>   *I was working. Then I stopped **to watch** TV.*

Sometimes the meaning is very similar:

*I like **watching** TV / I like **to watch** TV*
*I hate **seeing** cruelty to animals / I hate **to see** cruelty to animals.*

● The traditional rule is that *like* is usually followed by an *-ing* form, and that an infinitive is incorrect. Recent computer studies of spoken English indicate that the use of the infinitive in the examples above is nearly as frequent.

INVITATIONS

invite /ɪnˈvaɪt/ You ask someone to something, e.g. a party, your home, a movie

The function of inviting often includes *you*:

*Will **you** come to my party on Saturday?*
*Would **you** like to come?*
*Can **you** come?*
*Do **you** want to come?*
Please come to my party.

IRREGULAR VERBS

● Many of the most frequent English verbs are irregular in the past tense and past participle. You can find lists in dictionaries and grammar books. Try to learn verbs in groups with similar sounds or spellings.

Look in a dictionary, and find more verbs like the ones below.

no change	put / put / put
	cost / cost / cost
one change	keep / kept / kept
	have / had / had
two changes	drink / drank / drunk
	go / went / gone
two changes with -en ending for the past participle	eat / ate / eaten
	fall / fell / fallen
past participle the same as the infinitive	come / came / come
	run / ran / run

How many past participles do you know that have an /n/ sound at the end?

● Some verbs have a regular form and an irregular form:

learn / learnt / learnt
or
learn / learned / learned

● In American English, use the regular form. In British English you can use either. How many verbs can you find like this?

LET'S / LET ME

let's means *let us* (= allow us). *let's* is used for suggestions and arrangements:

Let's *go. /* **Let's** *meet at seven.*

let me is used for offers:

Let me *carry that for you. /* **Let me** *help.*

1   Make three arrangements with a partner.
2   Make three offers to help a partner.

LOCATION

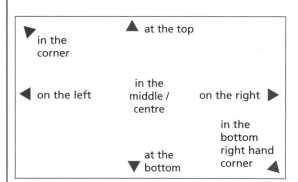

These are the location words we use for describing something which is vertical like a wall. If we are describing something *horizontal* like a table top, simply change *bottom* to *front* and change *top* to *back*.

This is a map of a street with six houses:

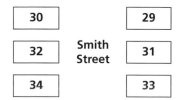

Number 30 is *opposite* number 29. Number 31 is *next to* (*next door to, beside*) number 29. In this street, all the even numbers are *on the left* (*left hand*) side and the odd numbers are *on the right* side. So number 32 and number 34 are *on the same side*. Number 31 is *between* number 29 and number 33.

Describe a room in your home, explaining the location of things in it.

LOOK + ADJECTIVE

In English we usually put adverbs after verbs. But after verbs of perception, we put adjectives. These verbs are *look, seem, sound, smell, taste, feel*. So we say:

> It looks **bad**, NOT ~~It looks badly~~.
> It sounds **interesting**. It smells **terrible**. She seems **nervous**. I feel **tired**.

Underline the verbs of perception in this text, then circle the adjectives after each of them.

> Big Muddy River are a rock group. Their new album sounds great! They look good, too. I feel relaxed when I listen to them. My favourite musician is the guitarist. He seems very shy, and he looks young.

MAY, MIGHT

● There is little difference in meaning between *may* and *might*.

might is the conditional form of *may*, and therefore sounds more polite when making requests:

> **May** I have a coffee?
> **Might** I have a coffee?

For requests and permission, *may* is much more frequent than *might*. Note that with requests and permission, the short answer is *may* for both *might* and *may*:

> **Might / May** I leave early today?
> Yes, you **may**. / No, you **may not**.

There are contracted negatives *mightn't* and *mayn't* but *mightn't* is rare and *mayn't* is very rare indeed. Use *might not* and *may not*.

● Both can be used to discuss future possibility:
> I **may** go to England next year.
> I **might** go to England next year.

For future possibility, *might* is more frequent than *may*. In American English, *may* is rare for talking about future possibility.

There is sometimes a small difference in meaning – *may* can mean something is more likely to happen than *might*:

possible	It may rain later.
possible but less likely	It might thunder later.
possible but very unlikely	It might even snow later.

MODALS

● Auxiliary verbs are used with other verbs to form questions and negatives, to give short answers, to add question tags and to indicate tense or time.

● Modal verbs are like auxiliary verbs in several ways – they are sometimes called modal auxiliary verbs. But modal verbs also add something to the meaning. Modals often show the speaker's feelings, opinion or judgement about what is being said.

These feelings involve:

– how certain the speaker is. These modals express certainty, probability, possibility, impossibility:
must / can't / may / might / could / shall / should / will / would
– the speaker's opinion on how free someone is to do something These modals express obligation, prohibition, permission, ability, lack of obligation, willingness:
must / mustn't / shall / will / need / can / need

● Modals are also used for requests, suggestions, advice, invitations, offers:
will / would / may / might / can / could

● Some verbs are 'semi-modals' – they can be used as modals or as ordinary verbs:
need / dare / used to

OBJECT PRONOUNS

Object pronouns are:
me / you / her / him / it / us / them

Subject pronoun	Verb	Object pronoun
He	is looking at	them.
They	know	us.
You	don't like	her.

Put object pronouns into the spaces.

1 That's my pen! Give it to ....
2 Mr and Mrs Gray? I don't know ....
3 She's very nice. I like ....
4 Jenny and I will be in the coffee shop at 11 o'clock. Can you meet ...... there?
5 I can't find my book. I put ...... over there somewhere.
6 I'd like to phone ...... later. Are you going to be at home?

OBLIGATION – MUST / HAVE TO

● In British English *must, have to* and *have got to* express obligation. In American English, *must* is only used for strong obligations. Use *should* or *have to* for weak obligations. The past tense is always *had to*. The future tense is *must* or *will have to*.

must is a modal verb:
> I **must** do it. **Must** I do it?

have to is a normal verb:
> I **have to** do it. She **has to** go.
> Do you **have to** go now?
> Does he **have to** catch a bus?

● *mustn't* is used for prohibition and warning:
> You **mustn't** do that!

needn't and *don't have to* are used when there is no obligation:
> Don't worry. You **needn't** do the homework tonight.
> You **don't have to** do the homework tonight.

● Most of the time there is no difference in meaning between *must* and *have to*. But when the obligation is external, we are more likely to use *have to*:
> The prisoners **have to** get up early.

When the obligation is internal or personal, we are more likely to use *must*:
> I **must** send my sister a birthday card.

As a result, *I have to go* (= I don't want to, but there is an external obligation) sounds more polite than *I must go* (= this is my idea).

Complete the spaces with *must, have to* or *has to*.

1 ...... you go now? The party's just beginning!
2 I don't ...... get up early tomorrow.
3 She ...... to wear a uniform at work.
4 I ...... phone my mother tonight.
5 Does he ...... to work on Saturdays?

OFFERS

Offers, suggestions and invitations often use *will / shall,* and the meanings are similar.

> **offer** /ˈɒfə(r) / You say or show that you will do something for another person, or give something to another person.

The function of offering often includes the words *I* or *me*:
> **I'll** do it (for you). Let **me** do it (for you). Shall **I** do it (for you)? Do you want **me** to do it? Would you like **me** to do it? Can **I** do it for you?

but also:
> Would you like a (drink)?

OUGHT TO

ought to means the same as *should* for giving advice and talking about weak obligation. It is sometimes said that *ought to* is stronger than *should*. You often see it with *they*:
> They **ought to** build more roads.
> The government **ought to** increase pensions.
> You **oughtn't to** eat so much fat.

See also **should** below.

PASSIVES

When we say what people and things do we use the active voice:
> Leonardo **painted** the Mona Lisa.

the Mona Lisa is the object of the verb *painted*. Our first interest is in the subject, Leonardo.

When we say what happens to people and things we use the passive voice:
> The Mona Lisa **was painted** by Leonardo.

The Mona Lisa is the subject of the passive verb *was painted*. Our first interest is in the painting, *the Mona Lisa*.

We form the passive by using the correct tense of ***to be*** + **past participle**:

active	passive
They make toys there.	Toys are made there.
They built it in 1089.	It was built in 1089.
They have done it.	It has been done.
They had lost the key.	The key had been lost.
They'll finish it soon.	It will be finished soon.
They can't do it.	It can't be done.
They should do it.	It should be done.
They are doing it now.	It is being done now.
They were helping them.	He was being helped.

Note that the passive sentence doesn't usually need to talk about an agent, i.e. the person or thing which did the action.
> The wall is being painted now.

If we are interested in the agent we can add *by* + an agent:
> The wall is being painted **by Doris Flambeau, the famous mural artist**.

Transform these sentences from active to passive.

1 They design the cars in Italy.
2 They built the car in Spain.
3 They have made 250,000 cars.
4 They will make 75,000 cars next year.
5 They are building a new model in Malaysia.

6 They can paint the cars by computer.
7 Last year they were testing the cars in the Himalayas.
8 They had tested several different designs.

PAST CONTINUOUS

The past continuous is also called the past progressive.

Affirmative and negative

I She He It	was wasn't was not	working	yesterday. last week. on Friday. at 7 a.m. in August.
We You They	were weren't were not		

Questions

Was	he she it I	working	yesterday? last week? on Friday? at 7 a.m.? in August?
Were	you we they		

Short answers

Yes, I was. / No, she wasn't.
Yes, we were. / No, they weren't.

Work with a partner. Find out what they were doing at these times yesterday:

6 p.m. / 7.30 p.m. / 9.17 p.m. / 10.52 p.m. / 11.59 p.m. / 1.05 a.m. today

PAST PARTICIPLE

We use past partciples in these constructions:

Present perfect	I've been there twice.
Past perfect	He'd done a lot of work.
Perfect of modals	I would have bought it, (if I had known.)
Passives	It's made in Belgium. They were sold last week.
Some adjectives	A well-oiled wheel, a white painted wall.

What are the past participles of these verbs?

1 go	5 fly	9 hear
2 know	6 fall	10 play
3 see	7 have	11 hit
4 drink	8 listen	12 do

PAST PERFECT

Affirmative and negative

I You He She We They	had 'd hadn't had not had	done it been there seen one met one travelled there gone that way	before. until then. at that time.

Questions

Had Hadn't	you he she they	done that been there seen one listened to it	before? then? at that time? in 1994?

Short answers

Yes, (I) had. / No, I (hadn't).

You can think of the past perfect as 'the past of the past.' When you report the past simple and the present perfect, the report will be in the past perfect for both tenses:

*I went there … He said (that) he **had been** there.*
*I have already seen it … She said (that) she **had** already **seen** it.*

PAST PERFECT CONTINUOUS

This is also called the past perfect progressive.

Affirmative and negative

I You We They	had hadn't	been	living there waiting working	for	a long time. two (weeks).
He She				since	1993. the previous (week). the (year) before.

Questions and short answers

Had you been waiting for a long time?
Yes, (I) had. / No, (I) hadn't.

Questions with *how long*?

How long had you been studying English?
How long had she been working there?

PAST SIMPLE

Affirmative and negative

I You She He It We They	went didn't go did not go	there at 3.15.	yesterday. last week.

Questions

Did Didn't	you we they I he she it	go work live	there?

Short answers

Yes, (I) did. / No, (she) didn't.

Many common verbs are irregular:
go / went; drive / drove; buy / bought

Other verbs are regular. We add *-ed* or *-d* to make the past tense:
walk / walked; like / liked

Remember, you don't need to know the past tense of a verb to make questions and negatives.

Write negative answers to the questions below.

1 Did you drive there?
   No, I didn't drive there.
2 Did she buy one?
3 Did they know her?
4 Did you fly there?
5 Did we see that programme?
6 Did you hear it?

Find the past tenses of these verbs.

see	buy	want	feel
give	get	swim	eat
drink	find	lose	sing
need	have	make	run

PERMISSION

● Conditional forms are more polite.

use	would	instead of	will
	should		shall
	could		can
	might		may

● Longer formulas are more polite:
I hope you don't mind me asking, but would you mind terribly if I opened the window?
is more polite than:
Can I open the window?

● A rising tone is more polite.

Asking for permission

Is it all right if May Can Could Might Do you mind if	I we	smoke? park here? leave early? look at your newspaper?

Giving and refusing permission

May I … ?	Yes you may. No, I'm afraid not. No, you may not. (very strong)
Can we … ?	Yes, you can. No, I'm afraid not. No, you can't. (strong)

If you ask with *could* or *might*, the answers will be with *can* or *may*:
Could *I open the window?*
*Yes, you **can**. / No, you **can't**.*
Might *I leave early?*
*Yes, you **may**. / No, you **may not**.*

Note that there is a contraction for *may not* (*mayn't*) but it is not used in American English and is very rare in British English. Use *may not*.

● *Do you mind if …?* is a little unusual. If you answer *yes* it means that you do mind, i.e. you will not give permission.
Do you mind if *I smoke?*
Yes, I do. *I'm sorry.*

If you answer with *no* it means that you don't mind, i.e. you will give permission.
> ***Do you mind if** I open the window?*
> ***No, I don't.** That's OK. / Not at all.*

POSSESSIVE ADJECTIVES

Possessive adjectives are sometimes called **possessives** or **possessive determiners** in recent grammar books. They are:
> *my / your / his / her / its / our / their*

Be careful of spelling, especially with *its*. Many English speakers make mistakes and write *it's* (perhaps because they think it is a possessive form like *Bill's house, Maria's car* etc.; perhaps also because *it's = it is* is so frequent that it's a habit to write it).

Put possessive adjectives in these sentences.

1 Excuse me! That's ...... book. Give it back to me.
2 There was a car with ...... engine on fire.
3 They bought ...... own house two years ago.

POSSESSIVES

- The possessive form of nouns is:
  *He's **Anna's** husband.*
  *That's **Mr Smith's** newspaper.*
  *That's **Sharon and Kevin's** house.*

For names ending in *-s*, we can use:
> *She was Prince Charles' girlfriend.*
or
> *She was Prince Charles's girlfriend.*

We can pronounce the second 's' or it can be silent in these examples.

- The possessive pronouns are:
  mine / yours / his / hers / ours / theirs

Rewrite each sentence using a possessive pronoun.

1 It's her car. It's hers.
2 It's their house.
3 It's our classroom.
4 They're his books.

PREPOSITIONS OF PLACE

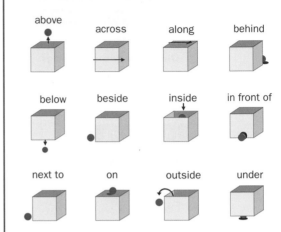

It is often difficult to know whether a word is a preposition of place or an **adverb of movement**. You needn't worry about it. In many books, they are put together because they have a similar idea.

PRESENT CONTINUOUS

The present continuous is also called the present progressive. We use it to describe things which are happening now. It is also used for talking about future plans and arrangements:
> *I'm flying to Rome tomorrow.*

Affirmative and negative

I	'm am 'm not am not	working. listening. doing it.
He She It	's is isn't is not	
We You They	're are aren't are not	

Questions

Are	you we they	listening? working? doing it?
Is she it	he	
Am	I	

Typical time words: *now / at the moment / right now* + future time words

Complete the spaces.

1 What ...... she doing?
2 He ...... n't listening.
3 ...... they watching TV?
4 It ...... raining.
5 Where ...... we going?
6 ...... you working?

PRESENT PERFECT SIMPLE

Affirmative and negative

I You We They	've have haven't have not	done it (yet). been there. seen it.
He She It	's has hasn't has not	

Questions

Have Haven't	I you we they	done it (yet)? been there? seen it?
Has Hasn't	she he it	

Short answers

Yes, I have. / No, they haven't.
Yes, she has. / No, he hasn't.

We use the present perfect:

● for actions beginning in the past and continuing up to the present (and possibly into the future). We use it for questions and negatives about experiences meaning 'until now':
  I've done a lot of work today.
  Have you ever eaten sushi?
  She's never been to England.
  Have you finished that book yet?

● for actions that happened at an indefinite time in the past, and which have some kind of result in or connection to the present. There needn't be a time word:
  Have you studied French?
  They've won!

● for recent actions:
He's recently started work at my company.
I've just cleaned my room.
It's OK. I've already had a drink.

● for repeated actions:
I've often been to France.
She's always done her work on time.

Typical time words: *already / just / yet / for / since* + present time words; frequency adverbs

PRESENT PERFECT V SIMPLE PAST

When we say that something *has happened*, we are thinking about the present and the past at the same time. The action started in the past, but there is a result or consequence in the present:
  I've lost my purse. (present perfect)

We know that the action losing the purse was in the past, but there is a consequence in the present (you don't have the purse now).

If you say *I lost my purse* (past simple) we don't know what the consequence is now. Maybe you don't have the purse, maybe you found it later and you have it now; the sentence gives us no information about 'now'.

PRESENT PERFECT CONTINUOUS

The present perfect continuous is also called the present perfect progressive.

Affirmative and negative

I You We They	have haven't	been	living here waiting wearing it working	for	a long time. two weeks.
He She	has hasn't			since	Monday. 7.15.

Questions and short answers

Have you been waiting for a long time?
Yes, (I) have. / No, (I) haven't.
Has he been helping you?
Yes, (he) has. / No, (he) hasn't.

Questions with *how long*?

How long have you been studying English?
How long has she been working there?

PRESENT SIMPLE

Affirmative and negative

I You We They	come don't come do not come	from England. to school every day. here by car.
She He It	comes doesn't come does not come	

Questions

Do Don't	you we they I	come work live	here?
Does Doesn't	she he it		

Short answers

Yes, (I) do. / No, (they) don't.
Yes, (it) does. / No, (she) doesn't.

Complete the spaces with *do, does, don't* or *doesn't*.

1 ...... it often rain in your country?
2 She ...... like tea at all.
3 ...... this train go to London?
4 ...... you know the way to the station?
5 I ...... like him at all.
6 We ...... live in Britain.

PRONOUNS

Pronouns can replace a noun in a sentence. See under the seperate headings for more information.

Subject pronouns	I, you, he, she, it, we, they
Object pronouns	me, you, him, her, it, us, them
Possessive pronouns	mine, yours, his, hers, its, ours, theirs
Reflexive and emphatic pronouns	myself, yourself, himself, herself, themself, itself, ourselves, yourselves, themselves
Demonstrative pronouns	this, that, these, those
Indefinite pronouns	something, anything, nothing somewhere, anywhere, nowhere etc.

QUESTION FORMATION

Questions with *is / are / am / was / were*

Statement	Question
She is tired.	Is she tired?
They were early.	Were they early?

Questions with modals

Statement	Question
They would like one.	Would they like one?
He must go.	Must he go?
They can swim.	Can they swim?
It will rain.	Will it rain?

Questions with the auxiliaries *do / does / did*

Statement	Question
He likes tennis.	Does he like tennis?
They live there.	Do they live there?
She went home.	Did she go home?

QUESTION TAGS

Question tags are used when we expect the listener to agree with us or to confirm the correctness of what we are saying. Question tags agree grammatically with the main part of the sentence. In some English varieties (e.g. in parts of Wales, Africa and India) there may be a single question tag for all tenses. Unfortunately, in mainstream British and American English you have to make the tags agree grammatically!

- Affirmative statements have negative tags:
  It's a nice day, isn't it?
  She knew him, didn't she?

- Negative statements have affirmative tags:
  It wasn't right, was it?
  You don't study French, do you?

Add question tags to these statements.

1 She's got a bad cold, ... ?
2 He doesn't understand, ... ?
3 We need some money, ... ?
4 You didn't hear me, ... ?
5 It started at seven, ... ?
6 They'd like to go home now, ... ?

Note that in American English you will often hear *You have a pen, don't you?* (agreeing with *Do you have ...?*). In British English you would usually hear either *You've got a pen, haven't you?* or *You have a pen, haven't you?*

● Intonation is important. Normally question tags have a falling tone at the end. A rising tone at the end means it is a real question and you are not sure of the answer.

Our train leaves from platform 14, doesn't it?

Try saying the sentences in this section first with a falling tone (checking), then with a rising tone (asking).

QUESTION TYPES

Closed questions

Purpose of question: checking information
Type of response: *Yes / No* response

Short closed question:
Did you work in France?

Tag question:
You worked in France, didn't you?

Statement with question intonation:
You worked in France?

Statement with *So / I see:*
So / I see you worked in France.

Information questions

Purpose of question: asking for specific information
Type of response: *Yes / No* response: limited response

Short closed question:
Did you work in France?

Long closed question:
Did you work in France or (did you work) in Germany?

Wh- question:
Where did you work last year?

Indirect question:
Can you tell me where you worked last year?

Open questions

Purpose of question: communication
Type of response: open response / free response

Open *Wh-* question:
How did you feel about working in France?
What did you think of France?
What things do you like about working in France?

Totally open questions:
Can you tell me about yourself?
What is the meaning of life?

REASON

● Clauses of reason answer the question *Why?* *because* is used before a clause with a subject and a verb.
because of is used before a noun or a pronoun:
*We got wet **because** it was raining. / **Because** it was raining, we got wet.*
*We got wet **because of** the rain.*

● After a question, a clause with *because / because of* can stand alone:
Why are you wet?
***Because** it was raining. / **Because of** the rain.*

● After the word *reason*, don't use *because / because of:*
*We missed the bus. That's the **reason** we were late.*

REFLEXIVE AND EMPHATIC PRONOUNS

● Reflexive pronouns are:
myself / yourself / himself / herself / itself / oneself / ourselves / yourselves / themselves

We use them when the subject and the object of the sentence are the same person:
*I hurt **myself**.*
*She taught **herself** German.*

They are often used for emphasis (meaning that person … not anybody else):
*He did it all **himself**.*
*I spoke to the Queen **herself**.*

Note that the second person has a singular form, *yourself* and a plural form, *yourselves*.

● Some verbs which are reflexive in other languages are not usually reflexive in English, e.g. *wash, dress, shave, feel, concentrate:*
*I usually **shave** before breakfast.*
*He can't **concentrate** on his work.*
*She **feels** ill.*

● We can use reflexives with *wash, dress, shave* when the action is unusual and we want to emphasize this:
*She's only two years old, but she can dress **herself!***
*Since his accident he can't shave **himself**.*

See also **each other** above.

Complete the spaces.

1   They built their house ....
2   It's automatic. It switches ...... off.
3   I like looking at ...... in the mirror.
4   John, I can't help you. Can you do it ...... ?
5   I hope you both enjoy ....
6   We didn't buy it, we made it ....
7   She taught ...... to play the guitar.
8   He cut ...... badly.

REGULAR VERBS

Regular verbs add *-ed* to form the past tense and past participle:

- Past tense:
  She called yesterday.

- Past partciple:
  I've called her three times.
  She is called Jen by her friends.
  A well-dressed woman.

- Spelling rules:

+ ed:
  want / wanted; need / needed,
  dress / dressed; seem / seemed

+ d:
  like / liked; love / loved; fade / faded

y to -ied:
  try / tried; apply / applied; cry / cried

double the consonant:
  *travel / travelled *; stop / stopped,*
  bat / batted; bug / bugged

  * But American English: *travel / traveled*

Write the past of these verbs.

1	kill	6	tape	11	pat
2	hate	7	hurry	12	die
3	fry	8	program	13	live
4	talk	9	play	14	chat
5	request	10	close	15	phone

Then write down a list of parts of the body. Write at least ten. You can make nearly all of them into regular past tenses by adding *d / ed*: *handed, elbowed, headed* etc.

You can make all of them into adjectives formed with past partciples: *well-armed, thin-lipped, big-eared*.

RELATIVE CLAUSES

Relative clauses give more information about the person, place or thing we are describing, and are used to combine sentences.

- There's a book in the library about Egypt. It is very interesting.
  *There's a book in the library about Egypt **which** is very interesting.*
  Do you know the people? They live next door to you.
  *Do you know the people **who** live next door to you?*

- Use *which* for things, *who* for people.
  You can replace both *which* and *who* with *that*:
  *There's a book in the library about Egypt **that**'s very interesting.*
  *Do you know the people **that** live next door to you?*

- You can also use *when* and *where* to introduce relative clauses:
  *I remember exactly **when** I first met him.*
  *I often think of the place **where** we first met.*

REQUESTS

Here are some ways of requesting things:
  A cup of coffee.
  A cup of coffee, please.
  Give me a cup of coffee.
  I want a cup of coffee.
  I'll have a cup of coffee.
  I'd like a cup of coffee, please.
  Can I have a cup of coffee?
  Could I have a cup of coffee?
  May I have a cup of coffee?
  Would you get me a cup of coffee?

Try saying all of the sentences (a) politely (b) rudely.

RESULT

Words which introduce clauses of result include *therefore, as a result, so that*.

- *therefore* is used in maths and science:
  $x = 3$ and $y = 5$. **Therefore** $x + y = 8$
  (We can use the symbol $\therefore$ for *therefore* in maths.)

- *therefore / as a result / so that* are used in formal arguments:
  *The company has lost money, **therefore** it will need to reduce costs.*

*The company has lost money. **As a result** (of this) it will need to reduce costs.*
*We are letting 100 employees go, **so that** costs will be reduced.*

See also *due to*, which does not appear in this course.

SEEING VERBS

see, watch, look at are often confused:

- *see* tells us about ability – either you can see or you can't see. It's almost never used with a continuous tense (except when it means 'meet').
- You *watch* something that is moving, e.g. a TV programme, a game, children playing.
- You *look at* something that is still, e.g. a painting, a beautiful view, a magazine.

Choose the correct verbs.

1 Can you (see / watch / look at) my car? There's something wrong with the engine.
2 It's very dark in here. I can't (see / watch / look at) anything!
3 Sorry, can I phone you later? I'm (seeing / looking at / watching) the news on TV.
4 'Please (see / watch / look at) the board,' said the teacher.
5 Ow! There's something in my eye. Can you (see / watch / look at) what it is?

SHOULD, SHOULDN'T

- *should* and *shouldn't* are modals. They are used for giving advice and for weak obligation:
  *You **should** eat less meat.*
  *You **shouldn't** drink so much.*
  *You **shouldn't** park on yellow lines in Britain.*

We use a perfect form to talk about the past:
*You **should** have told her.*
*She **shouldn't** have borrowed my car.*

- *should* is also the conditional form of *shall*. This is formal.

Type 1 conditional:
*If she forgets my birthday I **shall** be very upset.*
Type 2 conditional:
*If she forgot my birthday I **should** be very upset.*

See also **ought to** above.

Give advice with *should / shouldn't* to someone who wants …

1 …to lose weight (i.e. get thinner).
2 … to become very rich.
3 … to get a good grade in their exam.

SUGGESTIONS

suggest /səˈdʒest/ You say that something is a good idea. You say that someone should do something with you.

The function of suggesting often includes the words *we* or *us*:
*Why don't **we** go for a drink? Shall **we** have a cup of tea? Let's (Let **us**) go.*

SUPPOSED TO

There are several uses of *supposed to*:

- talking about regulations / prohibitions = *(not) allowed to / should(n't)*
  *You're not **supposed to** smoke in public buildings in California.*

- talking about general beliefs:
  *Too much cheese is **supposed to** be bad for you.*
  *Orange juice is **supposed to** be good for you.*

- contrasting what should happen with what actually happens:
  *You're not **supposed to** copy CDs onto tape, but a lot of people do.*
  *He was **supposed to** be at work today, but he's not here.*

See also **allowed to / permitted to** above.

TOO / VERY

- Look at these examples:
  It's very far, i.e. It's a long distance.
  It's too far i.e. It's a long distance. And so it is impossible for (us) to go there.

Remember:

- You cannot use *very* and *too* together (*It's very too far*)
  Do not use *too* when you mean *very*.
  *They're **too** cheap. (i.e. They're probably no good. I don't want them.)*

They're **very** cheap. (i.e. Great! I'll take ten of them.)

● *too* is often followed by an infinitive (*to do*), *for* or *for* + an infinitive:
I'm **too** tired to get up!
We're **too** late for dinner.
It's **too** cold for us to go to the beach.

UNLESS

You can think of *unless* as meaning *if … not.*

● Type 1 conditional:
The remote control won't work if you don't point it at the TV.
*The remote control won't work **unless** you point it at the TV.*

● Type 2 conditional:
I wouldn't stay in this job if I weren't happy.
*I wouldn't stay in this job **unless** I were happy.*

● Type 3 conditional:
He would have hurt himself if he hadn't jumped out of the way.
*He would have hurt himself **unless** he had jumped out of the way.*

WAS, WERE

Affirmative and negative

I She He It	was wasn't was not	here there at school ill busy	yesterday. last night. on Sunday. at 8 p.m. in July.
We You They	were weren't were not		

Questions

Was	he she it I	here there ill busy	yesterday? last night? on Tuesday? at 5.30? in May.
Were we they	you		

Short answers

Yes, I was. / No, she wasn't.
Yes, we were. / No, they weren't.

WHEN & FUTURE TIME

● What time will you phone me tomorrow?
I'll phone you when I get to the office.

This sentence is future in meaning. It has two parts: *I'll phone you* which has a future verb, and *when I get to the office* which uses the present simple. We cannot use *will* or *going to* in the second part of the sentence.

We can reverse the order of the two parts:
When I get to the office, I'll phone you.

Note that the verb in the *when* part is still in the present tense.

● There is a group of time words which operate in the same way as *when*:
*I'll read a book **while** I'm waiting.*
*I'll be there **before** you are.*
*We'll go out **after** this rain stops.*
*We'll wait **until** you get there.*
*I'll tell you **as soon as** I know.*
*We'll go out **if** this rain stops.*

The *if-* sentence is a type 1 conditional.

● Remember that the present perfect is also a present tense, and you can use it where the *when* part of the sentence is finished:
*When I**'ve finished** the job, I'll call you.*
*I'll be there after I**'ve finished** work.*
*We'll wait in the car park until you**'ve finished**.*

Choose the correct words.

1 Shall we go out (after / until) you've eaten?
2 He'll be there as soon as he (can / will be able).
3 I often leave the light on (before / while) I'm sleeping.
4 I (won't / don't) see you until you've finished work.
5 You'll need a ticket before you (will get / get) on the train.

WHETHER

● *whether* is similar in meaning to *if:*

Reporting:
*I asked **if** she could help / I asked **whether** she could help.*

Indirect statements and questions:
*I don't know **if** it's hers. / I don't know **whether** it's hers.*
*Do you know **if** there'll be a bus at 10.30? / Do you know **whether** there'll be a bus at 10.30?*

● We often use whether with …*or not*:
I don't know **whether** *it will rain or not.*

● We must use *whether*, not *if* in these examples:
- After prepositions:
They argued about **whether** *to install a coffee machine or not.*
- Before infinitives:
I don't know **whether** *to buy a new computer.*

WILL, SHALL

● *will* and *shall* are used for the future simple. They are also used for several 'non-future' uses, e.g. offers, suggestions, requests, expressing willingness, promises, invitations and arrangements. The contraction of both is *'ll. won't* is the normal negative contraction.

● *shall* is much more frequent in British English, but is formal. The negative *shan't* is not used in American English (in very formal examples you might see *shall not*) and is becoming rare in Britain. This is because you don't use contractions in formal situations.

See also **future simple** above.

WOULD HAVE DONE

This is the perfect form of would (See also *should, must have done* etc.). You will see it in type 3 conditionals:
If I had known, I **wouldn't have done** *it.*

We often use would have done with a conditional meaning without saying a complete type 3 conditional sentence:

A: *I heard a noise downstairs during the night. I didn't know what to do! What* **would** *you* **have done**?
B: *I would have phoned the police. I* **wouldn't have gone** *downstairs!*

● Note the pronunciation; as *would* and *have* both have contracted forms, either or both can be contracted:
I'd have called the police.
I would've called the police.
I'd've called the police.

Read this situation and make suggestions with *I would/ wouldn't have (done).*

> I was at a railway station 200 kilometres from home, and it was late. I was waiting to catch the last train of the day. I got to the ticket office to buy my ticket, and found that I didn't have any money! Someone had stolen it from my pocket / bag! I didn't know what to do!

WOULD ('D) LIKE

I'd like … means *I would like ….* It's very simple. It's the same in every person:
I'd like / you'd like / she'd like / he'd like / we'd like / they'd like

Negative

(I) **wouldn't like** *…*

Questions

Would *(you)* **like** *…?*

Short answers

Yes, (I) **would**. / *No, (I)* **wouldn't**.

Complete the spaces in this dialogue.

A: …… you like a drink?
B: Yes, I …… . Thank you.
A: What …… you like? Tea?
B: No, I don't like tea. …… like a coffee.

WOULD LIKE (SOMEONE) TO DO

I'd like a drink.
I'd like to go out tonight.
I'd like you to come with me.
My parents **would like** me to visit them this weekend.

You can replace *'d like* with *want* in the examples. How many 'sensible' sentences can you make from the box below?

I	'd like	you	to help	me.
We	want	them	to phone	us.
They		us	to meet	them.
You		me	to marry	you.
		her	to write to	him.
He	'd like	him	to tell	her.
She	wants			

Listening appendix

INTRODUCTORY UNIT
Requests

3 Intonation
1 Bring me a menu, please!
2 Excuse me, I wonder if I could see the menu, please.
3 May I have the menu, please?

4 Intonation: requests or commands?
1 Get me a drink, please.
2 Could you get me a drink, please?
3 Can I have the menu?
4 The menu, please.
5 I'd like some mineral water.
6 I'd like some mineral water, please.
7 May I have the bill?
8 The bill, please.
9 Could you get my coat?
10 I wonder if you'd be kind enough to get my coat, please.
11 I want two of those, please.
12 I wonder if I could have some of that, please?

Room service

1 Listening

ROOM SERVICE Good morning. Room service. This is Gary speaking. How can I help you?
WOMAN I'd like to order breakfast, please.
ROOM SERVICE May I have your name and room number?
WOMAN Easton. Sandra Easton. Room 416.
ROOM SERVICE What would you like today, Ms Easton?
WOMAN A tomato juice. Er … some muesli and a plain yogurt.
ROOM SERVICE Any bread?
WOMAN Yes. Could I have some toast?
ROOM SERVICE White or wholewheat?
WOMAN Wholewheat, please. Then I'd like some eggs … poached eggs with bacon.
ROOM SERVICE Anything else with that?
WOMAN No, thank you. That's fine.
ROOM SERVICE And would you like tea or coffee?
WOMAN Tea, please.
ROOM SERVICE With milk or lemon?
WOMAN Lemon.
ROOM SERVICE Is that everything?
WOMAN Yes, that's it.
ROOM SERVICE And when do you want that?
WOMAN As soon as possible.
ROOM SERVICE About twenty minutes?
WOMAN That's fine. Thank you.

UNIT 1
Introductions

4 Find the conversations
1
WOMAN Mr Granger, I'd like you to meet Nick Thomas, from our Boston office.
MR GRANGER How do you do, Nick.
NICK Pleased to meet you, Mr Granger.
MR GRANGER Please. Call me Philip.

2
MAN Sarah Dean?
WOMAN Yes.
MAN I'm Paul Hodges from Warner Graphics. How do you do.
WOMAN How do you do.
MAN Would you like to see our new catalogue?

Forms of address

1 Listening

DRIVER Yes?
POLICE OFFICER Could you switch off your engine, please, sir?
DRIVER Certainly, officer. Er, what's the problem?
POLICE OFFICER Is this your vehicle, sir?
DRIVER Yes, it is.
POLICE OFFICER What's the registration number, sir?
DRIVER Um, P341 DRU … no, P314 DRU.
POLICE OFFICER May I see your driving licence, sir?
DRIVER Of course. There you are, officer.
POLICE OFFICER And you are Mr Robert Samson?
DRIVER That's right.
POLICE OFFICER Would you get out of the car, Mr Samson?
DRIVER All right, but …
POLICE OFFICER Come this way … look at your rear lights.
DRIVER Ah, I see. One isn't working.
POLICE OFFICER That's right, Robert.
DRIVER Well, it was OK this morning … I'm very sorry, officer. I didn't know.
POLICE OFFICER There's a motorway service station two miles from here. I'll drive behind you to the services. You can get a new bulb there, Robert.
DRIVER Yes. Thank you, officer.
POLICE OFFICER That's all right, Bob. Just be more careful in future.

UNIT 2
Making the right noises

1 Listening

1

TEACHER What's the difference between a hexagon and an octagon?

STUDENT Um … a hexagon and an octagon … um …

TEACHER Go on.

STUDENT Er … a hexagon has six sides, and an octagon has … er … eight sides.

2

WOMAN What's the time?

MAN Eh?

WOMAN What's the time?

MAN The time! It's six o'clock.

3

SUE Hello, Phil. It's Sue.

PHIL Hi, Sue.

SUE I was just on the phone to Josh King.

PHIL Uh-huh.

SUE He's coming to London on Thursday …

PHIL Mm.

SUE … and I'm going to bring him to the meeting on Friday…

PHIL Uh-huh.

SUE I hope we'll see you there.

PHIL Yeah. Look forward to it. Bye, Sue.

4

MOTHER Katie said her first word today.

FATHER Really? What was it?

MOTHER She said 'Daddy'.

FATHER Aaah!

5

MAN This laser printer isn't working.

SUPERVISOR Let me see.

MAN I don't understand it.

SUPERVISOR It's simple. There isn't any paper.

MAN Ah! Sorry.

3 Misunderstandings

CLIENT My company needs forty million dollars for the new project.

BANK DIRECTOR OK.

CLIENT We're going to build a new office in Singapore.

BANK DIRECTOR Right.

CLIENT We can pay back the money – there's no problem with that.

BANK DIRECTOR OK.

CLIENT I can have my accountants call you next week.

BANK DIRECTOR Yep.

CLIENT So, we have a deal!

BANK DIRECTOR Yes … no! I mean I need some time. I'll get back to you.

4 Non-committal sounds

CLIENT My company needs forty million dollars for the new project.

BANK DIRECTOR Uh-huh.

CLIENT We're going to build a new office in Singapore.

BANK DIRECTOR Uh-huh.

CLIENT We can pay back the money – there's no problem with that.

BANK DIRECTOR Uh-huh.

CLIENT I can have my accountants call you next week.

BANK DIRECTOR Uh-huh.

CLIENT So, we have a deal?

BANK DIRECTOR I need some time. I'll get back to you.

UNIT 3
Checking information

1 Checking information on the phone

ALAN Computer Line. Alan speaking. How can I help you?

VICTORIA I want to order some software.

ALAN Do you have an account with us?

VICTORIA Yes, I do.

ALAN What's your post code?

VICTORIA BN3 9NL.

ALAN Bear with me. Ah, yes. Victoria Perry?

VICTORIA That's right.

ALAN And it's 18 Talbot Road, Brighton, isn't it?

VICTORIA That's correct.

ALAN And do you want to put this on your MasterCard?

VICTORIA Yes, I do.

ALAN Fine. What do you want to order, Victoria?

Saying the wrong thing

2 Listening

1

MS DRISCOLL Let's get straight to the point. Why do you want this job?

INTERVIEWEE 1 Well, I read the advertisement, and the salary is much better than I'm earning now.

MS DRISCOLL Is the money important to you?

INTERVIEWEE 1 Oh, yeah! It's important to everyone, isn't it? But it's not just that. I believe you have a lot of hotels in the Caribbean and the Far East, and that employees can get cheap holidays there …

2

MS DRISCOLL Ah, I see from your résumé that you've won several gold medals for ballroom dancing.

INTERVIEWEE 2 Yes, that's right.

MS DRISCOLL And you've been to several countries for competitions, including Japan.

INTERVIEWEE 2 Yes, I have.
MS DRISCOLL Mm. What did you think of Japan?
INTERVIEWEE 2 It was very nice.
MS DRISCOLL Would you like to work abroad?
INTERVIEWEE 2 Uh … I don't know.

3
MS DRISCOLL Are you still working at the Whitbury Hotel?
INTERVIEWEE 3 Yes, I am. But I want to leave.
MS DRISCOLL Why is that?
INTERVIEWEE 3 Well, the hotel isn't doing very well, and there are a lot of problems. Business is down.
MS DRISCOLL Oh, really? What are the problems?
INTERVIEWEE 3 The restaurant manager is absolutely useless. There have been so many complaints from guests! Last Saturday, this woman came into reception and she told me …

4
MS DRISCOLL Do you enjoy meeting people?
INTERVIEWEE 4 Mm. Yeah. Like, it's very interesting to, um … you know … I enjoy meeting, um, different, um people … you know what I mean. They're all, kind of, uh, so … like … um … well, um… interesting …

5
MS DRISCOLL You've worked in a bank for two years. Why are you interested in hotel reception work?
INTERVIEWEE 5 Well, I like meeting people and I have a lot of friends who work in the tourist industry. In fact, my friend Michael has just come back from Spain. He was a tour guide in Granada. He's told me so much about the tourist industry. Granada's getting very popular now. You can fly there from Barcelona and Madrid …
MS DRISCOLL Mm. Do you speak any foreign languages?
INTERVIEWEE 5 No, but Michael speaks brilliant Spanish, and he's going to teach me.

6
MS DRISCOLL Why have you had five different jobs during the last year?
INTERVIEWEE 6 I've had a lot of bad luck recently. Stupid things, really. One of the jobs was a long way from home, and my car broke down. Things like that, you know.
MS DRISCOLL Oh, I see.
INTERVIEWEE 6 Yeah, and then I was training to be a flight attendant, but I had motion sickness …

7
MS DRISCOLL … and are there any questions you'd like to ask me?
INTERVIEWEE 7 Uh, no. I can't think of anything.
MS DRISCOLL Would you enjoy working in reception?
INTERVIEWEE 7 I don't know. I think so. I don't know much about it, really.

Receiving information

7 Taking a message

OPERATOR Zoran Trading.
CALLER I'd like to speak to Mr Kennedy, please.
OPERATOR Do you mean Mr Trevor Kennedy in the accounts department, or Mr Nigel Kennedy in the sales department?
CALLER Uh, sales, please.
OPERATOR Hold the line. Trying to connect you.
SECRETARY Sales department? Can I help you?
CALLER Uh, yes. Mr Kennedy, please.
SECRETARY I'm sorry, Mr Kennedy's in a meeting at the moment. Can I take a message?
CALLER Yes. I have to speak to him about my order. We need delivery by Wednesday.
SECRETARY Oh. Can I take your name?
CALLER Stewart. I'm from Nexus International.
SECRETARY Right, Mr Stewart. Is that Stewart with a 'w' or a 'u'?
CALLER W. S-T-E-W-A-R-T.
SECRETARY Can you spell Nexus, please?
CALLER Yes, N-E-X-U-S.
SECRETARY Sorry. Is that an 'n' or an 'm'? I'm afraid the line isn't very clear.
CALLER N for November.
SECRETARY Thank you, Mr Stewart. Mr Kennedy should be free by lunch time. Can he call you back then?
CALLER I'll be back in my office at two.
SECRETARY Fine. I'll ask him to call you after two. Does he have your number?
CALLER I'm not sure. I'd better give it to you. 01425-416955.
SECRETARY I'll just check that. 01425-416955.
CALLER That's right. Thank you.
SECRETARY Thank you, Mr Stewart.

UNIT 4

Suggestions and invitations

1 Listening

CAROL … that's it, Sarah. We've finished. Are you flying back to England tonight?
SARAH No, actually, I'm not. I'm going to stay for a few days. I want to see the sights!
CAROL Have you been up the CN Tower yet?
SARAH No, not yet.
CAROL Oh, OK. I'm free tomorrow. I can show you around, if you like.
SARAH That's very kind of you, Carol. But it's Saturday. I don't want to take up your time …
CAROL It's no trouble. I'd enjoy it.
SARAH Well, if you're sure …
CAROL Of course! Now, would you like me show you the sights?
SARAH It sounds good. I'd enjoy that.
CAROL It'll be fun. Is ten o'clock OK?
SARAH Yes, that's great.

CAROL Have you been to the waterfront?

SARAH No.

CAROL I know a great restaurant. Shall we go there for lunch?

SARAH Well, er ... yes. OK.

CAROL Fine. Let's meet about ten.

Apologizing

4 Listening

1

NAOMI Hello?

JASON Hi! Naomi? This is Jason.

NAOMI Hi, Jason.

JASON Look, I'm having a party. Can you come?

NAOMI Yeah. I'd love to ... When is it?

JASON Tomorrow night.

NAOMI Tomorrow? Oh, sorry, Jason. I can't. I'm working tomorrow night.

JASON Oh.

2

TONY Hello. 761-5438.

JASON Tony? It's Jason.

TONY Jason?

JASON Jason Lonsdale.

TONY Oh, hi, Jace. Sorry. I didn't recognize your voice. What can I do for you?

JASON I'm having a party tomorrow. Would you and Helen like to come?

TONY Hold on, I'll speak to Helen ... Helen!

HELEN *(in the background)* What!

JASON Jace is having a party. Tomorrow.

HELEN Party?

JASON Yeah.

HELEN Where?

JASON Jace Lonsdale.

HELEN Oh, no!

JASON Right ... sorry, Jace. I'm afraid we can't. We're ... um ...

HELEN Having dinner with my boss.

JASON Having dinner with Helen's boss.

3

ANNABEL Annabel Granger.

JASON Hello, Annabel. It's Jason Lonsdale here. There's a party at my place tomorrow. You're invited.

ANNABEL I'm terribly sorry, Jason. I'd love to come, but I'm busy tomorrow.

JASON Oh, dear. Er, do you know Jenny's number?

ANNABEL No, sorry, I don't.

JASON Oh, well, it doesn't matter.

ANNABEL But I'll see her at work tomorrow. I'll tell her for you, if you like. What time's the party?

4

MR BROWNING Yes?

JASON Is that Mr. Browning?

MR BROWNING Yes. Browning here.

JASON It's Jason Lonsdale, Mr Browning. I'm having a party at my house tomorrow. Would you like to come?

MR BROWNING I'd like to, Jason, but I have another appointment. I can't come, I'm afraid.

JASON Oh, dear.

MR BROWNING Why didn't you ask me earlier, Jason?

JASON I'm sorry. It's my fault. The party was a sudden idea.

5

JASON Michael! How's things?

MICHAEL I'm fine. Who is this?

JASON Jason. Look, can you come to a party tomorrow? It's at my house.

MICHAEL Where's that?

JASON You know, Michael. 13 East Street.

MICHAEL 13 East Street ... what time?

JASON Eight o'clock.

MICHAEL That's very nice of you. Uh, what's your name?

JASON It's Jason ... sorry, that is Michael Leary, isn't it?

MICHAEL No, I'm afraid not. This is Michael Chumley. I'm afraid you've got the wrong number.

JASON Oh, no. Sorry to trouble you.

MICHAEL That's quite all right. Er ... I can still come to your party, can't I?

UNIT 5
Attentive listening

2 Listening

A: Hi, Tina. You look well.

B: Yes. We've just been to the Costa del Sol.

A: Oh. What was that like?

B: It was very good ... we rented a villa near Malaga for the first week.

A: Oh, really?

B: The weather was lovely, of course. We were on the beach every day. The children loved it.

A: Uh-huh.

B: It's the first time we've taken them to Spain.

A: Oh?

B: Then the second week we hired a car and toured around. That wasn't really a good idea. Well, you know what kids are like in cars.

A: Yeah.

B: They complained all the time, 'Are we there yet? Are we there yet?' And it was too hot for them ...

A: Right.

B: But Granada was wonderful. I wanted to spend more time there, but the children got bored, of course. And you know in the evenings Tim and I wanted to go out ... to restaurants, but the kids just wanted to stay in and watch TV ... we had satellite TV in the hotel.

A: I see.
B: So we had room service nearly every night. We couldn't take the children to a restaurant because they got so bored.
A: Mm.
B: They don't really like long meals.
A: No.
B: I think next time we'll go camping. It's better for the children, and cheaper too.
A: Mm.

3 Echoing

A: Oh, did I tell you? Last month we went to Florida.
B: Florida?
A: Yes. We stayed in Orlando for three weeks.
B: Three weeks?
A: That's right. We flew there on British Airways.
B: British Airways?
A: Yes. It was wonderful. We flew First Class.
B: First Class?
A: Yeah! We won the holiday in a competition.
B: A competition?
A: You know, the 'Find the Football' competition in the newspaper, and we got two thousand pounds!
B: Two thousand pounds!

4 Checking that you understand

I remember my first visit to England. It was 1995. I stayed in London // at a hotel on Oxford Street. // The Cumberland Hotel. // Oh, you know it. Great. It's really fantastic for shopping. My mom told me to visit Carnaby Street. // Because it was, like, really cool in the sixties. // She has this picture of her standing next to the street sign. // She's wearing these awesome jeans. So. I had my picture taken there. Right by the sign. // I guess it's not the same one. Then I went to Stratford-upon-Avon // and I saw a play by William Shakespeare. // It was Hamlet. I really enjoyed visiting there. Hey, look at the time. I'm late for class. Good talking to you guys. Bye.

UNIT 6

Looking at facts and figures

1 Figures

- fifty three per cent
- sixteen million
- two hundred and fifty three thousand four hundred and ninety one
- forty thousand square kilometres
- zero point five per cent or point five per cent
- three point seven two one
- three thousand seven hundred
- five point nine
- two billion

- four plus three equals seven
- six minus two equals four
- twenty five divided by five equals five
- thirty three times three equals ninety nine
- two and a half
- thirty three and a third

Making a story interesting

2 Adding detail

This happened to a friend of my sister's. A few months ago she went into the Red Lion restaurant in the High Street. She'd been shopping and was really thirsty, so she bought a bottle of Sunny Soda – you know, the drink that they advertise on TV all the time. Anyway, she drank it really quickly. When she'd finished she saw something at the bottom of the bottle. It was a dead mouse! She felt really sick and couldn't go to work for three days. She wrote to Sunny Soda, and put the mouse in the envelope. Well, they asked her not to tell the newspapers and they gave her five thousand pounds!

Humour

2 Listening

1
This is a true story. Queen Mary was Queen Elizabeth's grandmother. She was afraid of her granddaughter's dogs. Once she was at a garden party and Elizabeth gave her a dog biscuit to give to one of the dogs. Queen Mary was absolutely terrified of the dog, and quickly gave the biscuit to her neighbour, the Archbishop of Canterbury. He thanked her and ate it.

2
Good evening, ladies and gentlemen. It's nice to be here. I had a phone call at six o'clock yesterday morning. I'd just gone into the bathroom to clean my teeth. I always … well, nearly always … clean my teeth as soon as I get up. Anyway, why does the phone always ring when you're in the bathroom? I don't know. I answered the phone and it was Bill Hayter, your chairperson, and he asked me to come here and speak to you tonight …

3
A school inspector saw two little girls in the front row of a class and they were absolutely identical.
'You must be twins,' she said.
'No, miss,' they answered together.
'But you are sisters, aren't you?' she asked.
'Yes, miss.'
'And how old are you?'
'We're nine,' they said at the same time.
'Then you must be twins!' said the inspector.
'No, miss. We're triplets. But our sister's got flu.'

UNIT 7

Being a good listener

1 Conversation

A: I've been having problems recently.
B: I'm sorry to hear that. You sound worried.
A: Yeah, it's my job. It's been making me anxious.
B: Your job's been making you anxious.
A: That's right. I'm worried about the future.
B: The future?
A: You see, I'm afraid I'm going to lose my job.
B: Mm, what makes you feel that?
A: Well, I've got a new boss. And she ... you know ... she criticizes my work all the time.
B: Mm. It seems as if she doesn't appreciate you.
A: That's right! She doesn't! I've got three kids, you know!
B: You must feel worried about them.
A: Yeah, I'm worried about the friends they're hanging around with.
B: In what way?
A: Well you know ... their friends are no good. They get my kids into trouble.
B: Mm, can you give me an example?

3 Reflective listening

Complete conversation

A: That's it! I'm really fed up with this job.
B: You sound angry.
A: I wish I'd never come here!
B: I'm sorry to hear that.
A: I mean, why do I have to make the coffee for everyone?
B: You don't like making coffee.
A: The trouble is, I can't refuse to do it. I don't want to lose my job.
B: So you're worried about your job.
A: I mean, I've got good qualifications. It's just ... I shouldn't be making the coffee. And nobody ever says 'thank you'.
B: So you feel they don't appreciate you.
A: That's right! I guess I should be more assertive.
B: In what way?
A: You know, I should explain my feelings to Mr Smith.
B: You think that will make you feel better.
A: Yeah! I'm going to see him right now. Oh, and thanks for listening. You've been a great help.

Dealing with complaints

2 Listening

1
OPERATOR Hampshire Electricity?
CALLER The Manager, please.
OPERATOR Trying to connect you.
SECRETARY Mr Gordon's office.

CALLER Can I speak to the manager, please?
SECRETARY This is the manager's office. Can I help you?
CALLER I want to speak to the manager!
SECRETARY Is he expecting your call?
CALLER No, but I got a bill from you this morning and it's ...
SECRETARY Is this an account enquiry?
CALLER Yes, and I want to ...
SECRETARY I'll put you through to the accounts department.
CALLER But I ...

2
KEVIN Computer Supermarket. This is Kevin speaking. How can I help you?
CALLER Yes, I ordered a laser printer last week and ...
KEVIN Can I have your name, please?
CALLER Peter Johnson.
KEVIN Just a moment ... is your address 17 Brookside Close, Chester?
CALLER That's right.
KEVIN OK. What seems to be the problem, Mr Johnson?
CALLER Well, I opened the box, and there was no power lead.
KEVIN Oh, no. That's really annoying. I am sorry.
CALLER What should I do?
KEVIN Put everything back in the box. We'll replace the whole thing.
CALLER But when? I really need ...
KEVIN No problem, Mr Johnson. A courier will deliver a new one and pick up the old one at the same time. That'll be tomorrow afternoon. Is that convenient?
CALLER Yes. Right, that's fine.
KEVIN And our apologies for all the inconvenience.

3
CLERK Harper's Department Stores. Mail order department. Hold on ... Sorry about the delay. Can I help you?
CALLER Yes. I've got a problem with an order.
CLERK What's the order number?
CALLER Uh, JV400-933-24GKS. I ordered two chairs.
CLERK What's wrong with them?
CALLER Nothing's wrong with them. They haven't arrived.
CLERK Oh, dear. I am sorry. We've been having trouble with our computer system.
CALLER Well, when can I expect them? You've already taken the money from my credit card.
CLERK Oh. I see. Mm. They arrived at our warehouse three weeks ago. I'm surprised you haven't got them.
CALLER So am I. When am I going to get them?
CLERK You'll have to call the warehouse. I can give you the number. Have you got a pen?
CALLER Yes, somewhere ... right. What is it?

CLERK 01511-498054. They're closed at the moment. Can you call them between seven o'clock and seven thirty tomorrow morning? I'm sorry I can't help.

CALLER Oh, don't be sorry. I shall never buy anything from Harper's again.

CLERK Pardon?

4

CLERK Traffic department.

CALLER I want to make a complaint.

CLERK We don't deal with complaints here.

CALLER Who do I speak to then?

CLERK I don't know. It depends on the complaint.

CALLER It's about my parking ticket.

CLERK Parking ticket? You want the finance department.

CALLER I don't. I've just spoken to them and they told me to phone you.

CLERK Well, it's nothing to do with us.

CALLER You're the traffic department, aren't you?

CLERK Yes, but …

CALLER You have to deal with it then. I'm not making any more phone calls. I want it sorted out now. Your department's made a mistake …

CLERK There's no need to lose your temper with me.

CALLER Lose my temper? Who am I speaking to?

CLERK I've told you before. The traffic department.

CALLER No. You. What's your name?

CLERK We aren't allowed to give personal information.

CALLER For goodness' sake!

Difficult questions

2 A political interview

JOURNALIST Thank you, Minister. Julie Birdshill. Sunday News. My question is this. Is the government going to increase spending on education?

POLITICIAN I'm glad you asked me that. As you know we've spent more on education than the previous government.

JOURNALIST My question was about the future. Are you going to increase spending?

POLITICIAN This isn't a simple problem. You see, population figures are actually decreasing in a lot of cities.

JOURNALIST But do you intend to increase spending?

POLITICIAN Education is already a major part of the government's expenditure, and let me say at once that education is vitally important to this country's future. I believe that strongly.

JOURNALIST You still haven't answered my question, sir. What do you plan to do about future expenditure?

POLITICIAN I'm sure education will always be enormously important to our party, and we have no plans for reducing expenditure.

JOURNALIST Can we get back to my point, sir? Do you have any plans for increasing expenditure?

POLITICIAN I think I've answered your question. Could we have another question please?

JOURNALIST Excuse me, minister. But I'd like a direct answer.

POLITICIAN Really, I don't have time for this. There are other journalists here, you know. They want to ask questions too.

JOURNALIST I'm sure we all want an answer to my question. Does the government intend to increase education spending, or not?

POLITICIAN Well, er, not as such. But let me say that …

JOURNALIST Thank you, minister. You've answered my question.

POLITICIAN Have I? Oh, dear.

UNIT 8
Facts, deduction, speculation

1 Listening

JEFF I think it's really disgusting, Jim.

JIM Well, it doesn't seem fair, Jeff. Myrtle's worked here for fifteen years. Fifteen years pushing that trolley, and then they do this! They didn't have the decency to tell her to her face.

JEFF Disgraceful. How did she find out then?

JIM From some bloke in the accounts department. He said she'd lost her job.

JEFF What, just like that?

JIM Just like that.

JEFF How did he know?

JIM The post-boy told him. He said they were going to install vending machines.

JEFF How did the post-boy find out? Had he been reading old Marriot's letters?

JIM No. He'd heard Marriot talking to his secretary. Marriot said he was expecting some vending machines. Well, that can only mean one thing, can't it?

JEFF What's that then, Jim?

JIM Vending machines in, tea ladies out! After fifteen years!

JEFF So, they're putting vending machines in the offices, then.

JIM Oh, they won't stop there! They'll put them here in the factory as well.

JEFF What? That'll be the end of tea breaks! I'm going to speak to the union.

Understanding each other

3 Listen and match

MR MARRIOT Hello, Ms Hardie. Please take a seat.

MS HARDIE Good morning, Mr Marriot.

MR MARRIOT Now what can I do for you?

MS HARDIE I'm sure you know why I'm here.

MR MARRIOT No, I'm afraid not.

MS HARDIE The tea ladies are very upset about losing their jobs.

MR MARRIOT I don't understand. Where did you hear that?

MS HARDIE We know your plans. You want to replace the tea ladies with vending machines.

MR MARRIOT Excuse me, Ms Hardie. Let me get this straight. You're telling me that I'm going to sack the tea ladies and install vending machines all over the building.

MS HARDIE Yes, that's right. And we're not going to allow it. The factory workers are furious. I'm sure the office staff feel the same.

MR MARRIOT Now wait a minute, Ms Hardie ...

MS HARDIE You haven't consulted anyone.

MR MARRIOT Sorry, Ms Hardie. There must have been a misunderstanding. I am installing a vending machine here on the top floor. We often work very late up here. And a vending machine seemed like a good idea.

MS HARDIE Let me get this clear. You're saying that you're not going to sack the tea ladies, and you're only installing one vending machine.

MR MARRIOT Yes, that's right. No problem then.

MS HARDIE Well, thank you for your time, Mr Marriot. I'm glad we've sorted this out.

MR MARRIOT Thank you, Ms Hardie. Goodbye. Sharon, I want you to make some phone calls. Ms Hardie has just given me an idea.

Expressing opinions

1 Listening

1 Sharon Maxwell

I don't have a strong opinion on this. There are arguments for, and against. I hope that both sides can arrive at some sort of agreement or compromise. I agree that there are advantages to vending machines, but I disagree with some of Mr Elgin's reasons. Personally, I don't see why we can't have both systems in operation.

2 Jim Hewitt

It's disgraceful, that's what I think. Disgraceful. You think you can sack five people just like that. Myrtle's been with the company for fifteen years. She's been here longer than Marriot. What about loyalty, then? You'd probably like to replace us all with robots. Well, you won't get away with it. There'll be trouble on the factory floor. And that'll cost you!

3 Roz Hardie

We have heard the 'facts' from Mr Elgin. I've had a good look at Mr Elgin's 'survey'. It was biased. However, the main point here is the union agreement on consultation. If you look at section 15, sub-section 3, you will see that there must be consultation on job losses. Before there is any decision, there must be a consultation process. This has not happened.

4 Alistair Marriot

Let me emphasize this – there has been no decision yet, and there will be no decision without consultation. I am worried about the company's image. British customs, like the traditional tea break, seem old-fashioned to our foreign customers. Sometimes old traditions must give way to new technology. We live in a competitive world, and Mr Elgin has shown us that vending machines are cheaper and more efficient. However, our company has always had good relations with its employees and their opinions are very important to us. To sum up, no one is going to lose their job in the immediate future. However, we will set up a committee to explore alternatives.

5 Myrtle Hewitt

I've been doing this job for fifteen years. I know everyone very well. I do my best to keep everyone happy. I know that old Mr Greyson likes three spoonfuls of sugar in his tea and two chocolate biscuits. If I lost this job, I'd never get another one. I just couldn't afford to lose my job ... I don't know what I would do.

6 Daniel Elgin

My report shows that the beverage service operative system ... a-hem ... 'tea ladies' if you prefer the gender-marked term ... is inefficient and costs too much. My statistics demonstrate that vending machines would cost 30.67% less per annum, and would be easier to maintain. The results of my survey show that 78.2% of employees would prefer vending machines. My conclusion is that we should install them as soon as possible.

Glossary

aggressive /əˈgresɪv/ *adjective* using or showing force or pressure in order to succeed
an aggressive salesman

appreciation /əˌpriːʃiˈeɪʃn/ *noun* [U] the feeling of being grateful for something
We bought him a present to show our appreciation for all the work he had done.

argument /ˈɑːgjumənt/ *noun* **argument (with somebody) (about / over something)**
1 [C, U] an angry discussion between two or more people who disagree with each other
Sue had an argument with her father about politics.
2 [C] the reason(s) that you give to support your opinions about something
His argument was that if they bought a smaller car, they would save money.

assertive /əˈsɜːtɪv/ *adjective* expressing your opinion clearly and firmly so that people listen to you and take notice of you
to speak in an assertive manner

attentive /əˈtentɪv/ *adjective* watching, listening to or thinking about somebody / something carefully
an attentive audience

communication /kəˌmjuːnɪˈkeɪʃn/ *noun* [U] the act of communicating
verbal / non-verbal communication
Radio is the only means of communication in remote areas.

compliment /ˈkɒmplɪmənt/ *noun* [U] **a compliment (on something)** a statement or action that praises or expresses admiration for somebody
People have often paid her compliments on her piano playing.

compromise /ˈkɒmprəmaɪz/ *noun* [C, U] **a compromise (between / on something)** an agreement that is reached when each side allows the other side part of what it wanted
Unless the union and the management can reach a compromise on pay, there will be a strike.

confrontation /ˌkɒnfrənˈteɪʃn/ *noun* [C, U] a fight or an argument
Management wanted to avoid a confrontation with the unions because they were worried about a strike.

consult /kənˈsʌlt/ *verb* [T] **consult somebody / something (about something)** to ask somebody or to look something up in a book, etc. to get information or advice
You should consult a doctor if the symptoms get worse.

consultation /ˌkɒnsʌlˈteɪʃn/ *noun* [C, U] a meeting at which something is discussed
The measures were introduced without consultation.

conversation /ˌkɒnvəˈseɪʃn/ *noun* [C, U] informal talk
I had a long conversation with her about her plans for the future.

conversation filler /ˌkɒnvəˈseɪʃn ˈfɪlə(r)/ *noun* [C] small remark to help the flow of conversation
Conversation fillers give feedback from speakers to listeners.

criticism /ˈkrɪtɪsɪzəm/ *noun* [C, U] (an expression of) what you think is bad about somebody / something
The council has come in for severe criticism over the plans.

culture /ˈkʌltʃə(r)/ *noun* [C, U] the customs, ideas, civilization, etc. of a particular society or group of people
the language and culture of the Aztecs

curriculum vitae /kəˈrɪkjuləm ˈviːtaɪ/ (*abbreviation* CV) (also *American English* **résumé** /ˌresuˈmeɪ/) *noun* [sing] a short account of your education and work experience, often used when you are applying for a new job

defensive /dɪˈfensɪv/ *adjective* showing that you feel that somebody is accusing or criticizing you
When I asked him about his new job, he became very defensive and tried to change the subject.

echo /ˈekəʊ/ *verb* [T] **echo something (back)** to repeat or send back a sound
The tunnel echoed back their calls.
(figurative) *The child echoed everything his mother said.*

excuse /ɪkˈskjuːs/ *noun* [C]

excuse (for something / for doing something) a reason (that may be true or untrue) that you give in order to explain your behaviour
There's no excuse for rudeness.

feedback /ˈfiːdbæk/ *noun* [U] information about something that you have done or made which tells you how good or successful it is
We need some more feedback from the people who use our textbooks.

formal /ˈfɔːml/ *adjective* (used about language or behaviour) used when you want to appear serious or official and when you are in a situation in which you do not know the other people very well
'Yours faithfully' is a formal way of ending a letter.
She has a very formal manner–she doesn't seem to be able to relax.

formula /ˈfɔːmjulə/ *noun* [C] (*plural* **formulas** or **formulae** /-mjuliː/) (in language learning) a fixed expression; one where you don't need to understand the grammar of the individual parts of the sentence
Here you are. There you go.

function /ˈfʌŋkʃn/ *noun* [C] (in language learning) the way in which language is used
Socializing, giving information, and getting someone to do something for you, are all functions.

gesture /ˈdʒestʃə(r)/ *noun* [C] a movement of the hand, head, etc. that expresses something
The driver of the car in front made a rude gesture and drove off.

hesitation /ˌhezɪˈteɪʃn/ *noun* [C, U] a time when you wait because you are not sure
She agreed without a moment's hesitation.

impression /ɪmˈpreʃən/ *noun* [C] the effect that a person or thing produces on somebody else
She gives the impression of being older than she really is.

improvise /ˈɪmprəvaɪz/ *American English* /ˌɪmprəˈvaɪz/ *verb* [I, T] to play music, speak or act using your imagination instead of written or remembered material

It was obvious that the actor had forgotten his lines and was trying to improvise.

indirect /ˌɪndɪˈrekt; -daɪˈrekt/ *adjective* not mentioning something openly
She gave only an indirect answer to my question.

interrupt /ˌɪntəˈrʌpt/ *verb* [I, T] **interrupt (somebody / something) (with something)** to make somebody stop speaking or doing something by saying or doing something yourself
I'm sorry to interrupt but there's a phone call for you.

intonation /ˌɪntəˈneɪʃn/ *noun* [C, U] the rise and fall of the level of your voice while you are speaking

logical /ˈlɒdʒɪkl/ *adjective* according to the rules of logic; reasonable
As I see it, there is only one logical conclusion.

narration /nəˈreɪʃn/ *noun* [C, U] telling a story; the story that you tell

opinion /əˈpɪnɪən/ *noun* [C] **opinion (of somebody / something); opinion (on / about something)** what you think about somebody / something
She asked me for my opinion of her new hairstyle and I told her.
He has very strong opinions on almost everything.

passive /ˈpæsɪv/ *adjective* (used about the form of a verb or a sentence when the subject of the sentence is affected by the action of the verb)
In the sentence 'He was bitten by a dog', the verb is passive.

pause /pɔːz/ *verb* [I] **pause (for something)** to stop for a short time
to pause for breath

phonetic /fəˈnetɪk/ *adjective* **1** connected with the sounds of human speech
2 using a system for writing a language that has a different sign for each sound
the phonetic alphabet

phonetics /fəˈnetɪks/ *noun* [U] the study of the sounds of human speech

point /pɔɪnt/ *noun* [C] [sing] **1** something that you say as part of a discussion; a particular fact, idea or opinion
During the meeting she made some interesting points.

2 the point [sing] the most important part of what is being said; the main piece of information
She always talks and talks and takes ages to get to the point.

off the point not connected with the subject you are discussing

process /ˈprəʊses/ *American English* /ˈprɒses/ *noun* [C] a series of actions that you do for a particular purpose
the process of producing steel

reason /ˈriːzn/ *noun* [C, U] **reason (for something / for doing something); reason (why… / that…)** the cause of something; something that explains why something happens or exists
What's your reason for being so late?
Is there any reason why you couldn't tell me this before?

relationship /rɪˈleɪʃnʃɪp/ *noun* [C] the way that people, groups, countries, etc. feel about or behave towards each other
The relationship between the parents and the school has improved greatly.

sarcasm /ˈsɑːkæzəm/ *noun* [U] the use of words or expressions to mean the opposite of what they actually say. People use sarcasm in order to criticize other people or to make them look silly.
'No, you didn't take long to get ready. Only two hours,' she said with heavy sarcasm.

sequence /ˈsiːkwəns/ *noun* [U] the order in which a number of things happen or are arranged
The photographs are in sequence.

sexism /ˈseksɪzəm/ *noun* [U] treating a person unfairly, or thinking that they are inferior, because of their sex, e.g. thinking that only men can do certain jobs, such as being an engineer

sexist /ˈseksɪst/ *adjective* connected with or showing sexism
a sexist attitude to women

side /saɪd/ *noun* [C] the position, opinion or attitude of a person or group of people that is different from that held by another person or group of people
Do you believe his side of the story?

take sides (with somebody) to show that you support one person rather than another
Parents should never take sides when their children are quarrelling.

signal /ˈsɪgnəl/ *noun* [C] a sign, action or sound that sends a particular message
The flag went down as a signal for the race to begin.

signal /ˈsɪgnəl/ *verb* [I, T] (signalling; signalled; *American English* signaling; signaled) to make a signal; to send a particular message using a signal
The policeman signalled to the driver to stop.

situation /ˌsɪtʃuˈeɪʃn/ *noun* [C] (in language learning) the place and time where a conversation is happening

social /ˈsəʊʃl/ *adjective* to do with meeting people and enjoying yourself
She has a busy social life.

socialize also **socialise** /ˈsəʊʃəlaɪz/ *verb* to spend time with people when you are not working
I don't socialize with many of my colleagues.

status /ˈsteɪtəs/ *noun* [U] a high social position
The new job gave him much more status.

submissive /ˌsəbˈmɪsɪv/ *adjective* willing to obey other people

turn /tɜːn/ *noun* [C] [sing] the time when you must or may do something
Please wait in the queue until it is your turn.

take turns (at something) to do something one after the other
You can't both play on the computer at the same time. You'll have to take turns.

verbal /ˈvɜːbl/ *adjective* (formal) spoken, not written
a verbal warning

Extracts based on *Oxford Wordpower Dictionary.*

Oxford University Press,
Walton Street, Oxford OX2 6DP

Oxford   New York
Athens   Auckland   Bangkok   Bogota   Bombay
Buenos Aires   Calcutta   Cape Town   Dar es Salaam
Delhi   Florence   Hong Kong   Istanbul   Karachi
Kuala Lumpur   Madras   Madrid   Melbourne
Mexico City   Nairobi   Paris   Singapore
Taipei   Tokyo   Toronto

and associated companies in
Berlin   Ibadan

OXFORD and OXFORD ENGLISH
are trade marks of Oxford University Press

ISBN 0 19-457220-X

Acknowledgements

The authors would like to thank Barnaby Newbolt, for his
foresight and encouragement in getting this project under
way, and for his creative input during the writing stages.
Our personal thanks also to Helen Forrest for her superb
work throughout the editing stages, and Shireen Nathoo,
whose design ideas were vital in shaping the book from an
early stage.

We have benefited enormously from the distinctive talents
of Emily Andersen, Alison Findlay, Penny Mishcon, and
Valerie Mulcahy for the artwork, and Peter Marsh for the
audio recordings. We would also like to thank Cristina
Whitecross and Neil Wood for their editorial support and
advice.

*The publishers would like to thank the following for their
permission to reproduce photographs:*
Allsport: Mark Thomson; Bruce Coleman: Mark Boulton,
Andrew J Purcell, Hans Reinhard; Camera Press: Bernard
G Silberstein, Dennis Stone; Colorific!: Jim Pickerell;
Corbis - Bettmann, UPI; The Daily Mail © Southern News
Group; Eye Ubiquitous: Gil Hanly, Skjold; Ford Motor
Company Ltd.; The Ronald Grant Archive; Sally & Richard
Greenhill; Robert Harding Picture Library; Hulton Getty
Picture Collection; The Image Bank: Steve Niedorf, Luis
Castañeda; The Kobal Collection; Magnum; The Military
Picture Library: Robin Adstead; Paul Mulcahy; Paramount
Pictures / Channel 4; Quadrant Picture Library: M Simon
Matthews, Mark Wagner; Rex Features: Peter Brooker,
Capstick, Sean Harris, Lethikura OY; Science Photo
Library: Tom Van Sant, Geosphere Project, Santa Monica;
Shone / Gamma / Frank Spooner Pictures; Skyscraper
Productions / Channel 4; Bhasker Solanki / BBC; Sporting
Pictures (UK); Stills / Frank Spooner Pictures; Tony Stone
Images: Clayton Fogle, Charles Gupton, Stephen Johnson,
Will & Deni McIntyre, Michael Rosenfeld, Walter Schmid,
Robin Smith, Thomson & Thomson, Penny Tweedie,
Chris Windsor, Art Wolfe; Telegraph Colour Library: T
Craig; Tiger Aspect Productions Ltd.: Matthew Ford;
Topham Picturepoint; Peter Viney; Virgin Atlantic
Airways; Virgin Management Ltd.

Location Photography by
Emily Andersen

Still Life Photography by
Mark Mason

Illustrations by
Kathy Baxter, Stephan Chabluk, Phil Healey, Ian Kellas,
Stephen Lee, Ed McLachlan, Nigel Paige, Stephen Player,
Paul Sample

Design by
Shireen Nathoo Design

*The authors and publishers would like to thank the following
organizations for their help and co-operation in the
preparation of this book:*
The Churchill Hospital Oxford, Dixons Oxford, Heathrow
Airport, Jessops Oxford, Lloyds of London, Oxford Society
of Crowd Artists, Sainsburys Oxford, Salisburys Oxford

*The publishers would like to thank the following for
permission to reproduce copyright material:*
Falcon Games Ltd.; The Far Side © Farworks, INC./Dist.
by Universal Press Syndicate, for *Tarzan* and *Excuse me, my
brain is full*; The Far Side by Gary Larson is reprinted by
permission of Chronicle Features, San Francisco, Ca. All
rights reserved, for *What we say to dogs*; *Out to lunch* by
Leeds Animation Workshop; The Daily Mail © Southern
News Group, for adapted extracts and photograph taken
from article: 'My crusade, by the bogus traffic cop who
patrolled M25'; dictionary extracts based on Oxford
Wordpower Dictionary

Although every effort has been made to trace and contact
copyright holders before publication, this has not always
been possible. If notified, the publishers will be pleased to
rectify any errors or omissions at the earliest opportunity.

*The publishers would like to thank the following individuals
and institutions for their kind assistance and advice in the
preparation of this book:*
AFS, Roissy-en-Brie, France; AMCF, Colombes, France;
Anglo-French Services, Roissy-en-Brie, France; Aximedia
Idiomas, Madrid, Spain; Willie Baird; The British Council,
Milan, Italy; British School, Milan, Italy; The British
Institute, Florence, Italy; Cambridge Centre, Valencia,
Spain; Chambre de Commerce, Orléans, France;
COPROM, Liancourt, France; Ecole Nationale
d'Ingenieurs de St Etienne, France; English in Action,
Rezé, France; English Today, St Gregoire, France; Four
Seasons Language School, Hamatsu, Japan; Liz Hallifax;
IES Tiempos Modernos, Zaragoza, Spain; IBFFP, Brussels,
Belgium; I Go To School, Bruges, Belgium; ILC, Paris; ITC
Piagria, Viareggio, Italy; ITEC, Grenoble, France; IUT,
Cergy, France; Linguarama, Grenoble, France; Lothlorien
Language Training, Exeter, England; Lycée Philbert
Delorme, L'Isle d'Abeau, France; Lycée Tocqueville à
Cherbourg, France; Hilary Plass; Oxford Institutes Italiani,
Vicenza, Italy; Reine Formation, Versailles, France; SPAW,
Paris, France; Teach In, Rome, Italy; Université Libre de
Rueil-Malmaison, France.